SPIRIT-LED BIBLE STUDY

THE
KINGDOM
of
POWER

HOW TO DEMONSTRATE IT
HERE & NOW

SPIRIT-LED BIBLE STUDY

THE KINGDOM
of
POWER

HOW TO DEMONSTRATE IT
HERE & NOW

GUILLERMO MALDONADO

WHITAKER
HOUSE

THE KINGDOM OF POWER:
HOW TO DEMONSTRATE IT HERE AND NOW
(Spirit-Led Bible Study)

Guillermo Maldonado
13651 S.W. 143rd Ct., #101
Miami, FL 33186
http://kingjesusministry.org/
www.ERJPub.org

ISBN: 978-1-60374-885-8
eBook ISBN: 978-1-60374-887-2
Printed in the United States of America
© 2013 by Guillermo Maldonado

Whitaker House
1030 Hunt Valley Circle
New Kensington, PA 15068
www.whitakerhouse.com

1 2 3 4 5 6 7 8 9 10 11 ᴟ 20 19 18 17 16 15 14 13

Contents

About the Spirit-Led Bible Study Series

The Spirit-Led Bible Study series is a collection of diverse, stand-alone Bible studies designed for either individuals or groups. Each self-study course features either a scriptural theme or a particular book of the Bible. Readers can go beyond just reading the Bible to become engaged in its truths and principles, learning to apply them to everyday life in practical ways while growing in their understanding of God and deepening their relationship with Him. Jesus said, *"When He, the Spirit of truth, has come, He will guide you into all truth"* (John 16:13). Readers are encouraged to recognize that it is only through the indwelling Holy Spirit that we may truly understand the Scriptures and exhibit the life of Christ in our lives, and that we must intentionally rely on the Spirit in all our reading and study of the Bible.

INTRODUCTION

God is the Supreme Ruler of the universe, including our world, and He wants us to be active participants in spreading His kingdom on earth. *"The earth is the LORD's, and all its fullness, the world and those who dwell therein"* (Psalm 24:1). The kingdom of God is the life of God exercising its influence as the power of the Holy Spirit works through our humanity. Wherever God's kingdom governs, it is visibly demonstrated, and every work of Satan must depart because darkness cannot remain in the same territory occupied by God's light.

Many of us have heard teachings or read books about the kingdom of God, yet few of us have had a deep revelation and understanding of what it is, so we miss out on its truths and benefits. We fail to understand its potency for changing lives.

The Kingdom and the Church

To understand the kingdom of God, we must first realize that it is not the same thing as the church. Jesus spoke of the kingdom more than one hundred times, while He referred to the church only twice. Following His crucifixion and resurrection, Jesus remained on earth for forty days before ascending to heaven. What did He do during this time? He instructed His disciples *about the kingdom.* (See Acts 1:3.) Jesus is God the Son (fully God and fully Man), and after He fulfilled His mission on earth, God the Father established Him as Ruler over the world. As it says in Revelation 11:15, *"The kingdoms of this world have become the kingdoms of our Lord and of His Christ, and He shall reign forever and ever!"* God gave Jesus all authority in heaven and on earth. (See Matthew 28:18.) He is our Lord and King, and through Him, the kingdom of God is spread throughout the world.

The church is composed of those who have been redeemed through the death and resurrection of Jesus and who are called to expand His kingdom, just as Jesus did when He lived on the earth. God's invisible, eternal, and supernatural realm impacts the visible, temporal, and natural world by means of men and women who are born by the Spirit into His kingdom. The church is not the kingdom but rather the *agency* through which the kingdom is extended.

The kingdom of God is the manifestation of the spiritual realm that demonstrates His lordship, dominion, and will on earth.

The Kingdom of God and the Kingdom of Heaven

Another misunderstanding about the kingdom is the meaning of the phrase "kingdom of God" versus the phrase "kingdom of heaven." In Scripture, these phrases are often used interchangeably. Yet, even though they are similar, I believe each implies something specific. The kingdom of heaven is a spiritual location called "heaven," from which God rules and influences the earth and the entire universe. This is God's dwelling place, or atmosphere, where His throne, court of angels, elders, and so forth are found. (See, for example, Revelation 4:9–10.) The Father's seat of glory and power is surrounded by *unapproachable light*" (1 Timothy 6:16).

The kingdom of heaven is invisible, but it impacts the visible world as the kingdom of God. Everything that takes place on earth to advance the kingdom must first be revealed, declared, and decreed in heaven. The kingdom of God extends the dominion and authority of the King to the world. It is the realm where His will is obeyed, producing a heaven on earth. For example, each time Jesus announced the good news of the kingdom, sickness, sin, demons, poverty, and death could not remain.

The kingdom of God flows in us and through us by the supernatural power of the Holy Spirit, especially as we learn how the kingdom functions and as we act on its principles. We must light the way for people to see the kingdom of God, so they may experience the arrival of the kingdom in their own lives and receive personal transformation, healings, and miracles.

These Bible studies are not based on theories but rather on knowledge gained from personal experience. Everything that I teach in these pages, our ministry has experienced. Thousands of people have seen and heard the manifestations of God's kingdom through our ministry. In this course, you, too, will discover the nature of God's kingdom of power and learn how to enter into it so that you may see it demonstrated *today*—in the here and now!

How to Use This Study

Introduction

Welcome to *The Kingdom of Power*, one of the courses in the Spirit-Led Bible Study series. We are delighted that you have made the decision to dig deeper into God's Word. This course is designed as a stand-alone biblical study on the theme of God's kingdom in the now. The study may be completed independently by individual students, or it may be used in a group setting, such as a Bible study, a Sunday school class, a course on the foundations of the Christian faith, or a prayer group. For those who have read the author's book *The Kingdom of Power: How to Demonstrate It Here and Now* (Whitaker House, 2013), these studies will reinforce its major themes while providing further scriptural study and application of the topic.

Elements of Each Study

(Note: All the elements, combined, lead to a comprehensive understanding of the topics in the studies, so the student should endeavor to read and respond to each one.)

Scripture Verse or Passage

Each study begins with a Scripture verse or passage that highlights the topic.

Introduction

The author provides background, context, and/or other relevant information to set the stage for the lesson that follows.

Study Questions

Each study includes approximately 15 questions, with some questions having multiple parts. The questions are organized under sections that emphasize particular aspects of the topic. Each question is followed by a corresponding Scripture reference in parentheses that enables the student to answer it. If a Scripture reference has *a* or *b* after it (e.g., "John 3:16a" or "John 3:16b"), this means the answer is found in the first part of the verse, "a," or the second part, "b." The student should read the Bible verse or passage and then write the answer on the line(s) provided.

Reflections

Each lesson includes insights that the author has gleaned from his experiences with the kingdom of God in ministry or his study of the theme of the kingdom in God's Word. For example, the first study features "Reflections on the Kingdom as the Eternal Now."

Key Definitions

Definitions and explanations of key concepts related to the kingdom of God are provided at various points throughout the studies.

Thought-Provoking Statements

Periodically, statements for personal reflection are presented in bold italics.

Conclusion

At the end of each study, the author sums up the topic, provides additional information, and/or offers a challenge to the student.

Prayer of Activation

A prayer is provided to activate the student to live out the principles in the lesson, being spiritually empowered to serve God and expand His kingdom in the world. Group leaders are encouraged to offer the prayer on behalf of the students, while the individual student is encouraged to pray the prayer for himself or herself. (Individual students should adapt the prayers to the first-person singular.)

Action Steps

Action steps are listed to enable the student to apply the lesson to his or her life in practical ways.

Encounters with God's Kingdom

Each study concludes with a testimony about someone who has had a life-changing encounter with the power of God's kingdom. These testimonies come from the author's church, King Jesus Ministry, in Miami, Florida; affiliated churches; or the author's other ministry experiences.

Study Helps

Bible Version

The main Bible translation used for this study is the *New King James Version*. Other Bible translations are used periodically, and they are designated as follows:

(kjv): King James Version

(niv): *New International Version*

(nlt): *New Living Translation*

Answer Key

At the back of this book, answers to the study questions are listed under the titles of the studies in the Answer Key section. In addition, the various section titles for each study are included for easy reference. The student's answers should reflect the content of those provided in the Answer Key, although the wording may differ in varying degrees, depending on the nature of the question.

Study 1

THE KINGDOM OF GOD IS WITHIN YOU

"The kingdom of God does not come with observation; nor will they say, 'See here!' or 'See there!' For indeed, the kingdom of God is within you."
—Luke 17:20–21

Introduction

A kingdom is the influence, dominion, will, and lordship of a king or prince over a certain territory for the purpose of governing its inhabitants. There can be no king without a dominion and subjects. The kingdom from heaven—the kingdom of God—is His realm and His foundation of power manifested on earth, and it is a reality that we can receive and enjoy today. It is His dominion and lordship, in which He establishes His will here and now through the redeeming work of His Son Jesus Christ in the lives of His people. God governs over earthly territories, entities, and human beings; He rules over sickness, poverty, and oppression. He is sovereign over His spiritual enemy, Satan (the devil), who seeks to promote his realm of darkness in the world to counteract God's kingdom of light. Jesus brought God's kingdom to earth, and God calls believers, as the church, to continue to expand His reign in the world through our authority in Christ and our power in the Holy Spirit.

Study Questions

Part I: A Kingdom Bestowed from Heaven

1. What was the message Jesus proclaimed as He began His ministry? (Matthew 4:17b)

   _____

2. God's kingdom and Jesus' kingdom are one and the same. What did Jesus say about His kingdom, revealing that it did not have its origins in an earthly realm but in a heavenly, supernatural one? Complete the following:

   (a) John 18:36a: *"My kingdom is _____ _____ _____*

   _____."

(b) John 18:36b: "*…My kingdom is* _____ _____ _____*.*"

KEY DEFINITION: The Greek word for "kingdom" in the New Testament is *basileia*, which means "royalty," "rule," "a realm" (STRONG, G932), or "sovereignty," "royal power" (NASC, G932). It comes from the root word *basileus*, which relates to the idea of a "foundation of power" (STRONG, G935).

---

3. What did Jesus say is our heavenly Father's good pleasure to give us? (Luke 12:32)

   _____

4. When some religious leaders asked Jesus when the kingdom of God would come, what did Jesus reply? (Luke 17:21b)

   _____

The kingdom of God must first come within us, so that it may be manifested externally.

REFLECTIONS ON THE KINGDOM AS THE ETERNAL NOW

When Jesus preached about the kingdom, He referred to it mainly in the here and now, saying that it "*has come upon you*" (Matthew 12:28), "*has arrived among you*" (verse 28 NLT), or "*is at hand*" (Matthew 4:17). He taught relatively little about the kingdom as the eternal future. He expressed the concept as a present reality, where there is no past or future—just an eternal now. Jesus said that the kingdom was "*at hand*" because heaven was on earth. He didn't tell people to wait for death to enjoy the kingdom in heaven; His message was that the kingdom had arrived and could be received now! Being forgiven of our sin through Christ is just an entryway into God's kingdom, which is infinite, eternal, and of unlimited power. The kingdom brings everything each human being needs, such as salvation, healing, deliverance, prosperity, and purpose. It is to be experienced today, and it is to be applied to each circumstance we are undergoing at this moment.

5. Jesus told various parables about the kingdom of God. In one parable, He compared the kingdom to a treasure in a field. In another, He compared it to a pearl of great price. How did the main characters in these two parables respond toward what they had found? (Matthew 13:44b, 46b)

_____

_____

_____

Part II: Qualities and Character of the Kingdom of God

6. When the apostle Paul brought the *"gospel of the kingdom"* (Matthew 24:14) to the Thessalonians, he did not bring it in *"word only"* but also in three other ways. What were they? (1 Thessalonians 1:5a NIV)

_____

7. In what ways did Jesus demonstrate the kingdom as He taught and preached?

(a) Matthew 4:23b: _____

_____

(b) Acts 2:22a: _____

Each time the kingdom is preached, there must be a visible demonstration of God's power to heal the sick, deliver the captives and the oppressed, and save the lost.

8. What are three characteristics of God's kingdom? Complete the following:

Romans 14:17: *"For the kingdom of God is not eating and drinking, but*

_____ *and* _____ *and* _____ *in the Holy Spirit."*

Part III: How to Enter the Kingdom of God

+ **Be Born Again**

9. (a) What must happen for someone to enter the kingdom of God? (John 3:5)

_____

(b) To be "born of the Spirit" is to be "born of God." (See John 1:13.) What is our role in this process? (Romans 10:9)

_____

_____

(c) Complete the following:

John 1:12: *"But as many as _____ _____ [Jesus], to them*

He gave the right to become children of God, to those who _____ _____

_____ _____."

There is no entry into the kingdom of God except by the new birth.

REFLECTIONS ON THE HOLY SPIRIT'S ROLE IN GOD'S KINGDOM

When we put our faith in Christ, God gives us the gift of His Holy Spirit, and we become carriers of the kingdom of God, which is revealed in us and through us by the Spirit. The Holy Spirit is the Administrator and Executor of the kingdom. Without the Holy Spirit, there is no kingdom or government of God on earth. He is the only One who can reveal the things of the kingdom and of its King. (See, for example, 1 Corinthians 2:11–12.) Righteousness, peace, and joy are possible only where He operates.

The Holy Spirit is always at work in the lives of God's people who yield themselves to Him. He produces great spiritual activity, manifesting miracles, healings, signs, and wonders. If the Holy Spirit were to be removed from our midst, we would be left with only a theoretical, theological, and historical kingdom without power, one that would be unable to produce change or transformation in people.

+ **Repent Wholeheartedly**

10. There is a corresponding step we must take in this process of being born again and entering God's kingdom, which both John the Baptist and Jesus proclaimed. Complete the following:

    Mark 1:15b: "_____, and believe in the gospel."

    Matthew 4:17b: "_____, for the kingdom of heaven is at hand."

11. (a) What did Jesus say is a requirement for entering the kingdom of heaven? (Matthew 18:3)

    _____

    (b) What quality about the child did Jesus commend—a quality that would make a person *"greatest in the kingdom of heaven"*? (Verse 4a)

    _____

KEY DEFINITION: Repentance is not an emotion, although it may also be expressed through the emotions. Rather, when we realize our true, bankrupt spiritual condition before God, and the rebellious nature that has led us away from Him, repentance is the decision we make to turn 180 degrees and walk in the opposite direction—toward Him. Repentance involves a new frame of mind that effects a change in attitude and lifestyle.

Repentance is the unalterable condition for preparing to receive the kingdom and for being born into the kingdom.

Part IV: The Priority of the Kingdom

12. (a) What did Jesus teach us to pray to God the Father concerning His kingdom? (Matthew 6:10)

_____

_____

(b) To underscore the meaning of the above statement, where should we ask that God's kingdom should come and manifest? (Verse 10b)

_____

The kingdom of God is His will and dominion exercised on earth as it is in heaven.

---

13. (a) What did Jesus say we must seek first in our lives? (Matthew 6:33a)

_____

(b) What will be the result if we do this? (Verse 33b)

_____

(c) What kinds of *"things"* did Jesus indicate that God the Father would "add," or provide, for us—things that people often worry about obtaining? (Verses 31–32)

_____

14. What kind of kingdom are we receiving from God? (Hebrews 12:28a)

_____

15. (a) To whom did Jesus compare the person who hears His sayings about the kingdom and does them? (Matthew 7:24)

_____

(b) In this Scripture passage, the rains, floods, and winds depict the trials, temptations, and adversities of life. What happened to the house of the man who built on the rock, and what happened to the house of the man who built on the sand? (Matthew 7:25b, 27)

_____

_____

True Christianity is the power of God visibly manifested through His children.

Conclusion

God's kingdom is a reality that can be lived here and now. We, His children, are to manifest His will, lordship, and dominion on earth wherever we go. Heaven is the pattern, or model, that we need to bring to our environment. We are to "seize" whatever is in heaven and bring it to earth: health, deliverance, peace, joy, forgiveness, miracles, healing, prosperity, and so much more! As we depend on the realm of God, we can visibly bring forth whatever is needed. When the kingdom is a priority in our lives—when we worship God, serve others, heal the sick, testify of Jesus, deliver the oppressed, give offerings, and take the gospel wherever we go—all of our needs will be supplied. Receive the revelation in this Bible study and dare to make the advancement of the kingdom of God your priority, in the name of Jesus, and you will see miracles begin to take place. The invisible kingdom will manifest in the visible realm, bringing transformation to people's lives.

At my church and in my ministry travels, I have seen Jesus heal people of cancer, AIDS, hepatitis, arthritis, diabetes, lupus, bipolar disorder, schizophrenia, and much more. Many people have experienced creative miracles, such as receiving new organs where they were missing them, and the restoration of cleft palates. In the name of Jesus, people have been delivered from homosexuality, pornography, thievery, abandonment issues, witchcraft, and addictions, such as those to alcohol, prescription medications, and illegal drugs.

I encourage you to make a decision to manifest the kingdom everywhere you go. Where there is spiritual darkness, remove it; where there is sickness, cast out the spirit of infirmity. The kingdom of power is within you. The only thing you need to do is to demonstrate it here and now!

Prayer of Activation

The kingdom of God is entered by spiritual birth, and this *"new birth"* (1 Peter 1:3 NIV) gives us citizenship in it. We cannot enter the kingdom by being religious; by belonging to a denomination, ministry, or sect; by being affiliated with a particular philosophy; by knowing the theology of salvation through the cross; or by any other means. The Bible says *"all have sinned and fall short of the glory of God"* (Romans 3:23). A total separation from the curse of sin must take place; the umbilical cord of iniquity that connects us to sin and the rebellious nature must be cut. The kingdom is not a mere "remedy." It involves becoming a new creation. (See 2 Corinthians 5:17.)

God wants His kingdom to manifest in you. He wants His realm to extend to others through you, bringing righteousness, peace, and joy in the Holy Spirit. If you desire to be reconciled to God and are willing to submit to His government (see Isaiah 1:18–19), pray the following prayer of repentance and receive forgiveness so that you may enter into the kingdom of God in all its fullness:

Heavenly Father, I recognize that I am a sinner, and I repent of my lifestyle, which is contrary to You and Your kingdom. I turn away from all my sins and rebellion, and I desire to follow You wholeheartedly. With my mouth I confess that Jesus is the Son of God, and I believe in my heart that You, Father, raised Him from the dead. In the name of Jesus, I am "born of God." Let Your kingdom manifest in my life. Use me to spread Your kingdom wherever I go. Amen!

Action Steps

+ Daily ask God to give you a revelation of His kingdom, with its power and characteristics, so that you can demonstrate it to the world.

+ Repentance is an essential part of entering into and participating in the life of God's kingdom. Even if you have already received Christ, take time now to examine your life and repent wholeheartedly before God. Begin by thinking of ways in which you have lived independently of God by gratifying your sinful nature and living as you pleased—prioritizing your own desires and standards for personal gain and satisfaction. The power of the kingdom is available to those who have fully repented and renounced their rebellion against God. Then, and only then, can you claim His promises of salvation, healing, deliverance, righteousness, peace, joy, and prosperity. Constantly seek to renew your thoughts and ways in accordance with God's thoughts and ways, and daily submit your life to Him, so that you will continue to walk in the right direction. For our repentance to be genuine, we must place ourselves, from this day forward, under God's authority and government, allowing Him to have full reign in our lives. When we live to please the King, we will not do anything without His consent, authority, and guidance. This is true repentance.

- ◆ Read Matthew 10:7–8 and begin to demonstrate God's kingdom! Throughout the New Testament, we read of the kingdom being brought to earth. You are a carrier of God's kingdom who is able to visibly manifest His power here and now. When you encounter people who are sick or in need of deliverance, remember that sickness and oppression do not exist in heaven. Therefore, "pull" the kingdom of heaven to earth, with its health and freedom in Christ, so that God's power can manifest and people can be healed and set free in the name of Jesus!

ENCOUNTERS WITH GOD'S KINGDOM

The Creative Miracle of a Brand-New Eye

Apostle Maldonado was ministering at a meeting in Dallas where many miracles and healings took place under God's anointing. Pastor Damion of Phoenix, Arizona, was in attendance. He is under the covering of a church associated with King Jesus Ministry, and he testified of a miracle involving a woman in his congregation. This woman's stepfather lives in Detroit and worked for an electric company. He had been beaten with a metal pipe because he had refused to do something illegal in relation to his job. As a result, his right eye had to be removed, and the eye area was sutured shut. Pastor Damion received a phone call from the woman in his congregation asking him to please keep her stepfather in prayer.

This pastor had been teaching his congregation some of the principles in Apostle Maldonado's book *How to Walk in the Supernatural Power of God.* One Sunday, he was moved by God to play a recording of one of King Jesus Ministry's services, which he downloaded from the ministry's Web site. He had remembered Apostle Maldonado mentioning something about playing such recordings during a service, because the spirit of healing and deliverance would remain in the atmosphere, producing additional healings and deliverances for those with the faith to receive them. After a powerful time of worship, Pastor Damion played the recording in faith, with the expectation that something would happen. Toward the end of the recording, Apostle Maldonado prayed, and during this part of the church service, the woman felt God prompting her to place her hand over her right eye as a prophetic act to accelerate the healing of her stepfather in Detroit. She believed, and the rest of the church believed with her, that something would happen.

Thirty minutes after the church service ended, Pastor Damion received a phone call from this woman, who was screaming into the phone. He thought something bad had happened, but she said, "The eye is back!" This is what had transpired: That morning, her stepfather was still in the hospital, and when the doctor was checking his sutures, he noticed something moving under the sutured eyelid. The doctor said that couldn't be, so they opened it up, and there was an eye! This man was able to see shapes and shadows, such as a newborn baby sees before his vision is fully developed. Later, he was able to see perfectly. God had created a new eye where the other one had been removed due to the severe damage it had sustained.

The stepfather was not a believer, but after this powerful miracle, he got saved and is now on fire for God. What's more, the man's stepdaughter has been able to become pregnant, after having been told by her doctors that she couldn't have children. In addition, the man's other daughter, who lives in Detroit, was healed of Crohn's disease. This is what the kingdom of God produces as it is demonstrated on earth!

Study 2
THE ORIGINAL MANDATE OF DOMINION

"Be fruitful and multiply; fill the earth and subdue it; have dominion over the fish of the sea, over the birds of the air, and over every living thing that moves on the earth."
—Genesis 1:28

Introduction

God's plan of expanding His kingdom throughout the earth through human beings did not begin with our redemption in Jesus. It is an eternal purpose, and His plan has been in effect since before the beginning of time. After creating the physical world and the animals, God made man and woman as the crown of His creation and put them in charge of manifesting His glory on this planet as His representatives and ambassadors.

God's will was for heaven to be duplicated on earth. He invested human beings with His power and authority so they could have dominion in three primary areas as they expanded His kingdom in the world: (1) rulership over creation, (2) power to perform all the works God called them to do, and (3) authority over Satan, demons, and any other evil spirits. Human beings were to rule over nature, space, time, and matter. They were to be kings over creation.

Study Questions

Part 1: Created to Have Dominion

1. In what manner did God make man (male and female)? (Genesis 1:26a, 27a)

_____

KEY DEFINITIONS: The word *"image"* in Genesis 1:26 is translated from the Hebrew word *tselem*, which can mean "resemblance" or "representative figure" (STRONG, H6754); it also has "the sense of essential nature" (VINE, H6754). The word *"likeness"* is from the Hebrew word *demuwth*, which can mean "resemblance," "similitude" (STRONG, H1823), "shape; figure; form; pattern." This word "signifies the original after which a thing is patterned" (VINE, H1823). *The Living Bible* best captures the sense of Genesis 1:27: *"Like God did God make man."* Since we were created out of the essence of God, we have His "genes." We are not "gods"; we are not divine. However, we have God's nature and characteristics. He created us in His lineage.

Mankind is intended to make of earth what heaven is like.

2. (a) God is an invisible, eternal Being, with supernatural abilities and attributes that are infinitely superior to the natural world. What is God in His essence? (John 4:24a)

    _____

    (b) What is the essential part of us as human beings, which will return to God after we die, as distinct from our bodies, which will return to the ground as *"dust"*? (Ecclesiastes 12:7b)

    _____

3. What were God's first instructions to Adam and Eve after He blessed them? Complete the following:

    Genesis 1:28a: *"God said to them, '_____ _____ and

    _____; _____ _____ _____...."'*

The prevailing principle of the kingdom of God is permanent expansion.

4. What did God plan *"beforehand"* for us to do as new creations in Christ that would enable us to "be fruitful" in the earth? (Ephesians 2:10a)

    _____

5. What are two other elements of God's mandate to humanity? Complete the following:

Genesis 1:28b: "…*fill the earth and* _____ _____; _____

_____ _____…*every living thing that moves on the earth.*"

KEY DEFINITIONS: In Genesis 1:28, the word *"subdue"* is translated from the Hebrew word *kabash,* which literally means "to tread down" and conveys such ideas as "conquer," "subjugate," "bring into bondage," "force," "keep under," and "bring into subjection" (STRONG, H3533). *Subdue* is a term often related to military power that indicates the force to overcome or bring under control. The word *"dominion"* is translated from the Hebrew word *radah,* and this word, also, means "to tread down." It has such connotations as "subjugate," "come to have dominion," "prevail against," "reign," "bear rule," "rule over" (STRONG, H7287), and "dominate" (NASC, H7287a). Many of these senses imply compelling someone to do something by force, to place underfoot, or to enslave. These words largely refer to the subjugation of Satan and his works.

Dominion is the highest spiritual power given to man, because it is territorial power.

---

6. Into what "territory" on earth did God first place human beings so they could *"tend"* and *"keep"* it? (Genesis 2:15)

Part II: Understanding Dominion

Exercising dominion involves both leading and ruling. We are leading when people follow us of their own free will and give us permission to guide them. We are ruling when people do not want to follow us, even though they may know we are carrying out God's will. When we rule, we have to make decisions that go against people's feelings and desires, in order to be obedient to God.

7. (a) Jesus demonstrated the pattern of kingdom leadership in John 13:3–17. What did He say we should do for one another (symbolically and sometimes literally), emphasizing the importance of servant leadership? (John 13:14b)

(b) In Matthew 20:25–28, Jesus contrasted the kingdom perspective of greatness with the worldly perspective. How did the rulers of the Gentiles, who were "great" according to the world's standards, treat those who were under them? (Matthew 20:25)

_____

(c) What did Jesus say about true greatness and what it means to be *"first"* among other people? (Verses 26b–27)

_____

_____

_____

We lead by means of spiritual fatherhood, relationships, service,
and example when people follow us willingly.

---

8. (a) We cannot exercise "leadership" over our spiritual enemy, the devil, since he will never change his evil ways. Instead, we must rule over him. What is one way in which we are to do this? Complete the following:

   James 4:7: *"Therefore submit to God. _____ _____*

   _____....."

   (b) How will Satan react to this? (Verse 7b)

   _____

REFLECTIONS ON DOMINION

Men and women were created to *have dominion over* their environment; they were not designed to *be dominated*, to be controlled and suppressed. God did not design us to live like this, and it has no part in our dominion mandate. Jesus came to earth to restore human beings to dominion so we could rule over sicknesses, adverse circumstances, and Satan and his demons; so we could have power over alcohol addiction, drug abuse, bad thoughts, and anything else that causes us to move away from God's will. Moreover, dominion was not given to us so that we could subdue other human beings—only the enemy. If God gives us authority in other people's lives, it is only to govern, guide, and direct them, never to put them under subjection. Governing often requires great wisdom and self-control. We are to serve people and lead them into the blessings that God pours out upon the obedient.

---

9. (a) What is one way in which Jesus exercised rule during His earthly ministry? (Mark 11:15–16)

_____

_____

_____

_____

(b) In Jesus' subsequent teaching, what did He say to explain His actions? (Verse 17)

_____

_____

We rule with authority over those who are under our care but who refuse to follow us, as God's representatives, of their own free will.

---

10. The apostle Paul dealt with a situation of sexual immorality in the Corinthian church in which a man was openly sleeping with his father's wife and was unrepentant. The church was looking the other way instead of addressing the issue. Paul's instruction was to put this man out of fellowship with the church in hopes that he would be forced to come to his senses and repent, and thereby be spared the judgment of God. (See 1 Corinthians 5:1–5.) The Corinthians followed Paul's advice, and the discipline

worked. Yet the Corinthians turned out to be so zealous in their rule that they continued to shun this man even after he had repented. What did Paul tell them to do at that point? (2 Corinthians 2:7–8)

_____

_____

_____

11. What reason did Paul give Titus for rebuking those in the church who were rebellious and idle talkers, and who were deceiving people in regard to the truth of the gospel? (Titus 1:13b)

_____

12. Why does God chasten, or discipline, us? (Hebrews 12:10b)

_____

Conclusion

Human beings were designed to *"have dominion,"* or to rule. They were created as God's legal representatives to apply or enforce His kingdom laws on earth. After creating Adam and Eve, God put them into the garden of Eden, which was the environment of His presence. The garden of Eden was the base of operations, or starting point. From the garden forward, they were to expand God's rule throughout the earth, bringing His glory with them. The mandate God gave humanity began with *"Be fruitful and multiply; fill the earth…."* Here we see the concepts of both our calling to expand and our representation of God's image. The principle of multiplication is eternal. Human beings were meant to continue to fill the earth with God's kingdom through succeeding generations born from Adam and Eve and their children. God's kingdom is a limitless kingdom. It is an ever-expanding realm. It has always existed, it exists now, and it will continue to exist throughout eternity as it expands in ways we cannot now know or imagine.

To enable human beings to fulfill their role in the kingdom, God gave them a built-in desire and ability to lead and rule. He designed them with the ability to think, to address challenges, and to be creative, and He gave them the desire to exercise their power. This is why every human being has the instinct and need to exercise power in some form.

However, no one person, alone, could *"fill the earth and subdue it"* (Genesis 1:28). The dominion mandate is therefore a collective mandate. *Together*, human beings were to fill the earth and subdue it, each performing the unique purpose for which he or she had been created, as they all worked in unity to fulfill God's purposes. In a similar way, through our redemption in Christ, God has assigned each of us a portion of "territory," or "territorial power," where we can exercise the measure of our dominion on earth. This dominion is based on the faith, anointing, and gifts He has given to bless us and to further His kingdom.

Prayer of Activation

Father, Your Word says in Ephesians 2:10, *"For we are His workmanship, created in Christ Jesus for good works, which God prepared beforehand that we should walk in them."* We ask You to activate us in the dominion works You have prepared for us as we expand Your kingdom in our "territory," or sphere of influence, on earth. Let us exercise leadership with grace and apply rule with discernment. In Jesus' name, amen.

Action Steps

- What good works has God placed in your heart to do? Write them down and take action each day toward fulfilling them.

- Whom might God have placed in your life to receive the benefit of your servant leadership? Determine how you will fulfill your role using the pattern of servanthood Jesus provided.

- Whom has God placed in your life who needs firm but loving "rule"? Determine how you will respond to this challenge, keeping in mind that the ultimate goal is to help people be established in their faith and become more like God.

ENCOUNTERS WITH GOD'S KINGDOM

Supernatural Church Growth and Miracles

Paulo DaSilva is one of Apostle Maldonado's spiritual sons. Although Paulo was raised in a Christian home in Brazil, by the age of sixteen, he had lost his way. He spent two years involved with drugs, lies, and violence until he had a personal experience with God and returned to church. He studied theology, became a pastor, and worked hard to win souls, so that his congregation grew to 450 members. But stagnancy set in, and his church stopped growing. Instead of having joy and energy, he felt sad and tired.

Then, he discovered the supernatural power of God's kingdom, and as he demonstrated it, God released growth in his church. He now has over 1,300 active members, and he baptizes hundreds of new believers every month. His ministry has also established six new churches in Brazil in less than two years. The miracles he is seeing are amazing. God is healing people of cancer, AIDS, and various other infirmities. Marriages are being restored, and people are being delivered from addictions and are experiencing financial prosperity. The youth of the church are now on fire for God, ministering the supernatural everywhere they go. And the leadership of the church is being transformed as people learn to walk in kingdom power. You can do the same!

Study 3
Dominion Relinquished and Regained

"For this purpose the Son of God was manifested, that He might destroy the works of the devil."
—1 John 3:8

Introduction

To understand why God gave Adam and Eve dominion power over Satan at the beginning of creation, and why they fell from this dominion, we must look at Satan's background and motivations. He had been created by God as an angel called Lucifer, or "light." However, he rebelled against God and was expelled from heaven, along with a third of the angels who had joined him. Some theologians and Bible scholars have concluded that Satan's rebellion and expulsion from heaven took place between the first two verses of Genesis 1—between *"In the beginning God created the heavens and the earth"* (verse 1) and *"The earth was without form, and void; and darkness was on the face of the deep"* (verse 2). It is from this viewpoint that we will examine humanity's dominion mandate.

Satan had already been expelled from heaven when Adam and Eve were created, and his kingdom of darkness and destruction was in operation. The devil had seized the territory of earth, and God allowed him to do this—for His own purposes. It is essential to recognize that Satan is never stronger than God. He is a created being, and he was thrown out of heaven after he rebelled. God always has total control over everything He creates.

Genesis 1:2 says that *"darkness was on the face of the deep,"* meaning that the earth was in chaos and darkness because Satan had seized it; the presence of his kingdom always results in such disorder and destruction. But Genesis 1:2 also says, *"And the Spirit of God was hovering over the face of the waters."* Even in the midst of the darkness, God's power to create was present, because the territory of earth did not belong to Satan. He was a usurper. Under the influence of God's Spirit, the earth received light, order, and life. God made human beings and gave them dominion not only over the natural world and everything in it, but also over the enemy, who was still present on the earth. They were to subdue him and his kingdom— to bring him under control by spiritual force.

Yet the devil desired to shroud the earth in darkness once again. To do this, he had to recover his rule by taking the territory away from man, since God had granted man authority over it. Satan's plan was to make human beings fall from the glory of God by means of rebellion and disobedience—the same way by which he had fallen. So, he "prowled around" the earth, seeking to devour God's supreme creation. (See 1 Peter 5:8 NIV.) In a tragic decision, human beings chose not to use their authority over the enemy, and this is the origin of mankind's myriad problems. Yet God, in His sovereignty, would fulfill His purposes even in the midst of Satan's plan of destruction.

Study Questions

Part I: How Mankind Fell from Dominion

1. (a) Amid the other trees in the garden of Eden, what two special trees had God placed there? (Genesis 2:9b)

    _____

    (b) What command did God give Adam (and, through him, to Eve) about the trees in the garden? (Verses 16–17)

    _____

    _____

    _____

2. What did Satan, in the form of a snake, falsely insinuate that God had said? (Genesis 3:1b NIV)

    _____

3. (a) What lie did Satan tell Eve in regard to eating from the tree of the knowledge of good and evil? (Genesis 3:4)

    _____

(b) What did Satan say would happen to Eve if she ate the fruit? (Genesis 3:5b)

_____

_____

4. (a) How did both Adam and Eve respond to the serpent's suggestion? (Genesis 3:6b)

_____

(b) Why was Adam held more responsible than Eve for succumbing to Satan's temptation and sinning against God? Complete the following:

1 Timothy 2:14: "*Adam was _____ _____, but the woman _____ _____, fell into transgression.*"

5. (a) What were some consequences for the earth and for Adam (and all human beings to come) of Adam's sinning knowingly? (Genesis 3:17b–19)

_____

_____

_____

_____

(b) What are the *"wages of sin"*? (Romans 6:23a)

_____

A person's disobedience is the devil's legal authorization to attack him.

REFLECTIONS ON SURRENDERED DOMINION

When Adam disobeyed God, Satan made himself the earth's legitimate governor—legitimate not because God gave him this authority but because Adam sinned, thereby surrendering his authority to the kingdom of darkness. Consequently, human beings lost their dominion and their life in the presence of God. What is more, they lost the territory God had given them, and they entered into Satan's bondage. In essence, Adam gave the enemy the keys to his life, and that is how Satan took over the rulership of the earth.

6. How should Adam have responded to Satan's temptation, as Jesus responded to Satan's temptation given through Peter? (Matthew 16:23)

_____

_____

Part II: The Four Stages of Adam's Fall

  ✦ **Stage #1: Adam Was Aware of His Coexistence with Evil**

7. Which tree in the garden of Eden indicated the existence of evil? (Genesis 2:9)

_____

Coexisting with evil isn't the same thing as tolerating it.

  ✦ **Stage #2: Adam Began to Tolerate Evil**

8. (a) Recall in what manner Adam and Eve had been created. (Genesis 1:26–27a)

_____

(b) What idea from Satan did Adam and Eve entertain that led to their downfall? (Genesis 3:5)

_____

_____

9. In a comparable example of spiritual negligence from the New Testament, for what reason did Jesus admonish the church at Thyatira? (Revelation 2:20 NIV)

_____

_____

_____

The evil you tolerate will become the evil that destroys you.

+ **Stage #3: Adam Lost the Fear, or Reverence, of the Lord**

10. (a) When a person has the fear of the Lord, what will he hate? (Proverbs 8:13a)

_____

(b) What are some examples of this hated thing? (Verse 13b)

_____

<u>KEY DEFINITION</u>: To "fear the Lord" is to reverence, honor, and respect Him. It means to be in awe of Him. Thus, it guards us against yielding to evil. When Adam became indifferent to the dangers of evil, he soon entered into a relationship with it. If we lose our reverence for the Lord, evil will not be held back. God's Word tells us that if we fear the Lord, we will hate evil—we will not allow it to influence us.

Losing the fear of the Lord leads to a loss of sensitivity to evil; we no longer see its dangers and consequences, and we compromise the truth.

+ **Stage #4: Adam Finally Sinned**

11. (a) What leads us to succumb to temptation? (James 1:14b)

_____

(b) When an evil desire is conceived, what does it give birth to? (James 1:15a)

_____

(c) When sin is full-grown, what does it bring forth? (Verse 15b)

_____

REFLECTIONS ON ADAM'S DESCENT INTO SIN

Adam went from coexisting with evil to tolerating it to losing the fear of the Lord to falling from God's glory into the curse of sin. Today, the same sad descent and subsequent surrender to temptation takes place in the lives of millions of people. The strategy of the deceiver is to wear us out mentally, emotionally, and physically until we finally give in and fall. Satan and his demons observe us and know our weaknesses. They wait for the opportune moment to tempt us in our weakest area, often by deceit, until we lower our guards and submit. Satan discussed God's commandments with Adam and Eve in a way that was intended to confuse them and weaken their spiritual resistance. The devil will not stop trying until he sees you fall down or recognizes that you have the ability to resist him, so do not argue with him or entertain his ungodly suggestions. You must rebuke him—cast him out—immediately! Regardless of how logical or good those ungodly thoughts or arguments might seem as you try to rationalize them, remember that Satan's goal is always to destroy you.

Part III: The Catastrophic Result of Adam's Sin

12. (a) What designations did Jesus and the apostle Paul use for Satan, reflecting his role as usurper of Adam's earthly dominion? (John 12:31b; 2 Corinthians 4:4a KJV)

    _____

    (b) List some of Satan's qualities and motivations. (John 8:44b; Revelation 20:10a; John 10:10a)

    _____

    _____

13. (a) After Adam and Eve sinned, human nature was altered—it became "carnal" rather than being in alignment with God's Spirit. How is the *"carnal mind"* described? (Romans 8:7a)

_____

(b) What is the carnal mind not subject to? Complete the following:

Romans 8:7b: *"…it is not subject to* _____ _____ _____

_____, *nor indeed can be."*

(c) What statement did Paul make about the universality of humanity's fallen state? (Romans 3:23)

_____

(d) List some of the "works" of humanity's fallen nature. (Galatians 5:19–21a)

_____

_____

_____

_____

(e) What will not be inherited by those who practice the works of the fallen nature? (Verse 21b)

_____

The devil's plan was to contain Adam and Eve in sin, keeping them from expanding God's glory throughout the earth. He tries the same thing with us today.

Part IV: Jesus Restored Humanity to Dominion

By God's decree, dominion over the earth had been given to human beings. This is why Satan had to defeat Adam, a man, in order to rule the world. It is also why Jesus had to come to earth as a Man to destroy the works of the devil and conquer him forever. Jesus defeated Satan to demonstrate that it is possible for a human being to overcome temptation through the power of the Holy Spirit. Through the Spirit, Jesus accomplished what Adam had failed to do.

14. For what purpose did Jesus, the Son of God, come to earth as a Man? (1 John 3:8b)

_____

15. (a) What method did Jesus consistently use to resist the devil's temptations, in contrast to Adam's response, which was to tolerate, and, later, succumb to, temptation? (Luke 4:4, 8, 12)

_____

(b) How did the devil react when Jesus maintained His authority over him in each temptation? (Verse 13)

_____

(c) After His victory over Satan's temptations in the desert, in what manner did Jesus return to begin His mission of proclaiming the gospel of the kingdom? (Verse 14a)

_____

16. (a) After Jesus' resurrection from the dead, what statement did He make, showing that He had won back dominion of the earth from Satan? (Matthew 28:18b)

_____

(b) What did Jesus say to explain the authority He would grant believers? (Matthew 16:19)

_____

_____

_____

(c) What did Jesus come to earth to bestow on us? (John 10:10b)

_____

Ruling in the spirit realm starts with ruling our own spirit.

Conclusion

Because of humanity's fall from dominion and broken relationship with God, people's lives have become dominated by many harmful things, such as drugs, bad habits, a lust for money, an unhealthy desire for fame, and the torment of demons. Human beings are mainly dominated by their own fleshly desires. They went from being God's governors on earth to being ruled, manipulated, and controlled by the enemy of their souls. Yet, ever since Jesus' resurrection, Satan has been functioning as an illegal ruler on earth. More than that, his power has been defeated. He no longer has authority over us, unless, like Adam, we grant it to him. In each temptation and circumstance we face, we have the choice of defeating the enemy or giving in to him. When we give in to him, we allow him to gain a foothold in our lives.

What Jesus accomplished for us is powerful: it enables us to defeat Satan in the midst of our difficult circumstances in a fallen world. If we know our identity in Christ and are willing to cast Satan out of our "Eden," the enemy cannot defeat us. We must not tolerate sickness, sadness, depression, poverty, fear, or any other evil strategy designed to destroy us. We must be prepared to subjugate and dominate every work of the devil. Let us live in the reality that our dominion has been regained and that God's kingdom will continue to increase for all eternity!

Prayer of Activation

Heavenly Father, release over us the spirit of dominion that Jesus regained for humanity in order to bless us and to give us the power to spread Your kingdom throughout the world, pushing back the kingdom of darkness. We wholeheartedly ask that Your kingdom would begin to reign in our lives right now. May we rule over the entire "territory" of dominion that You have given us, beginning with our own spirit, soul, and body. Amen!

Action Steps

+ If you have allowed the devil to invade your "Eden," ask yourself some hard questions: "How did the enemy gain a foothold in my home life, finances, or business? Have I stopped tithing my income and ceased honoring God with my money?" "How did Satan afflict my body with sickness or disease? Have I tolerated a sickness or mistreated my body so that it became ill?" "How did Satan invade my church, city, or nation? In what way has my community given the enemy the legal right to afflict us?" Seek God with integrity and humility, and He will give you the answers. Then, repent and allow the blood of Jesus to cleanse you. (See 1 John 1:7–9.) Recover your Eden and take back the dominion rights the enemy has stolen from you!

+ What sins and wrong elements are you tolerating in your life—evil thoughts, attitudes, actions, and habits; people who are detrimental to your spiritual and emotional health; and so forth? Realize that, through them, you are giving the enemy the right to erode your fellowship with God and undermine your dominion, whether it is dominion over your character, your attitudes, or your behavior. Take back your God-given rule over addictions to alcohol, illegal drugs, or prescription pills; take authority over sickness, illicit sex, fear, depression, anger, bitterness, unforgiveness, a spirit of suicide, bickering, or gossip. Right now, renounce and rule over these things in the power of Christ. God has given you dominion over all of Satan's works and over the sinful nature.

ENCOUNTERS WITH GOD'S KINGDOM

Miraculous Healing of Cancer

Not long ago, Apostle Maldonado traveled with his ministry team to bring the supernatural power of God to the city of East London, South Africa. Hundreds of people convened at one of the churches there, and sitting among the audience at one of the meetings was Penelope Quluba, a woman who had been diagnosed with colon cancer three years earlier. Doctors had told her that the cancer was aggressive and could not be removed. They also said she would eventually become paralyzed and experience kidney failure. The only option was to put her on radiation and chemotherapy and let the cancer take its course. In addition, Penelope had to undergo surgery to have a colostomy bag inserted. As a result, she felt self-conscious because not only was she sick; she also carried an unpleasant odor.

After her diagnosis, Penelope regularly spoke healing over herself, declaring the Word of God and telling her body that it was the temple of the Holy Spirit and had not been created with aggressive cancer or a colostomy bag. By the time of the meeting in East London, she was due to have more surgery because she had completed the chemotherapy, and the doctors needed to see what was happening in her colon. Apostle Maldonado gave an altar call for those who had cancer or HIV. Penelope made her way to the altar, where the apostle laid hands on her and declared her healed in the name of Jesus. Two weeks later, when she visited the hospital for the first time since the ministry event, the doctors were baffled when they found no trace of cancer! They removed the colostomy bag and put everything back to normal. Penelope is now free of cancer and full of vitality by the grace of God.

Study 4

JESUS' RESURRECTION ESTABLISHED HIS KINGDOM AND DOMINION OVER THE KINGDOM OF DARKNESS

"God also has highly exalted Him and given Him the name which is above every name,
that at the name of Jesus every knee should bow…."
—Philippians 2:9–10

Introduction

After Jesus died on the cross for our sins to redeem us to God, He was gloriously raised from the dead. He continues to live today—and will live forever—to give life to all who believe in Him. Through His resurrection, Jesus validated His deity, His kingdom, and His dominion over Satan's kingdom. The resurrection marked a line between Satan's dominion over the earth and Christ's conquest of Satan, His eternal reign, and the reestablishment of mankind's dominion over the earth.

We can reign with the same power that raised Jesus from the dead! Resurrection power saves, heals, and delivers. As we receive the revelation of Christ's resurrection and truly live in it, we will witness miracles, signs, wonders, and the raising of the dead, advancing God's kingdom on earth as it is in heaven.

Study Questions

Part I: Jesus Experienced Three Kinds of Death on Our Behalf

Jesus' life on earth was an act of substitution—to restore our relationship with the Father and to restore our dominion—that reached its climax on the cross, where He died in our place for our sins. To be our Substitute, Jesus had to undergo the three types of death that every human being was destined to endure (without His redeeming work on the cross) due to Adam's rebellion and the sin nature inherited by the whole human race.

✦ Physical Death

1. What did Jesus *"taste"* in our place, so that we could receive eternal life? (Hebrews 2:9b)

   _____

2. (a) By what manner of execution did Jesus die? (Luke 23:33a)

   _____

   (b) What did Jesus say just before breathing His last breath? (Verse 46b)

   _____

3. When Jesus died on the cross, what did God lay upon Him? (Isaiah 53:6b)

   _____

In the exchange that took place at the cross, Jesus endured the consequences of our disobedience so that we could receive the benefits of His obedience.

✦ Spiritual Death: Separation from God

4. What did Isaiah tell the Israelites that their iniquities and sins had done to their relationship with God? (Isaiah 59:2)

   _____

   _____

5. What did Jesus say while He was on the cross, indicating that taking our sins on Himself had separated Him from His fellowship and union with God the Father? (Matthew 27:46b)

   _____

6. Why did God make Jesus, who had never sinned, to be sin for us? (2 Corinthians 5:21b)

   _____

Only sin, or iniquity, can separate a person from God.

+ **The "Second Death": Eternal Separation from God's Presence**

7. (a) What did Jesus say to describe how the Son of Man (Jesus) would spend the period of time between His death and His resurrection? (Matthew 12:40b)

_____

(b) Psalm 88 may be a prophetic account of Jesus' sufferings, including His thoughts toward God the Father as He suffered the "second death" in Sheol. How did Jesus describe His experience of God's punishment for the sins of humanity? (Psalm 88:6–8)

_____

_____

_____

REFLECTIONS ON THE "SECOND DEATH"

After Jesus died, His spirit descended into hell. In the Bible, the afterlife is sometimes called "Sheol," or "Hades." In Jesus' parable of the rich man and Lazarus, Hades is described as being divided into two regions: a place of torment (where the spirits of the unbelieving awaited their final judgment) and *"Abraham's bosom"* (where the spirits of the righteous awaited the completion of the Messiah's mission of salvation, so they could dwell in God's presence). (See Luke 16:19–31.) Jesus underwent the torment in Hades, or Sheol, that we should have received. He received each judgment in His spirit. Though Christ's suffering on the cross was horrendous, His spiritual suffering in hell, of which few believers seem to be aware, was even more terrible. He endured the wrath of God in the spirit realm for the sins and iniquities of the entire human race in order to save us from that place of torment.

8. What revelation had Jesus been given, as stated in the Psalms, concerning the state of His soul and His physical body after He died? (Psalm 16:10)

_____

_____

The resurrection is the manifestation of God the Father honoring His Son.

Part II: Jesus Experienced Two Resurrections on Our Behalf

+ **He Was Made Alive in His Spirit**

9. How was Christ spiritually resurrected following His death? Complete the following:

1 Peter 3:18b: *"Christ…being put to death in the flesh but made alive* _____ _____

_____*."*

Romans 6:4: *"Christ was raised from the dead* _____ _____ _____

_____ _____ _____*."*

10. To what group did Jesus "preach" after His spiritual resurrection but before His physical resurrection? (1 Peter 3:19b)

_____

KEY DEFINITION: The word *"preached"* in 1 Peter 3:19 is translated from the Greek word *kerusso*, which means "to herald (as a public crier), especially divine truth"; it indicates "to proclaim" and "to publish" (STRONG, G2784).

---

11. (a) To whom did Jesus preach *the gospel* before His physical resurrection? (1 Peter 4:6a)

_____

(b) What was His purpose in preaching to this second group? (1 Peter 4:6b)

_____

REFLECTIONS ON JESUS' SPIRITUAL RESURRECTION

Jesus was vivified, or made alive, in His spirit by the working of the Holy Spirit before His physical body was raised from the dead. The power of God came upon Jesus' spirit, which was instantly made alive. That was the initial resurrection He experienced. By the same power, we will all be resurrected one day! (See Romans 6:5.)

Jesus visited two groups after His spiritual resurrection. I interpret *"spirits in prison"* in 1 Peter 3:19 to mean evil spiritual entities, or demons. As God's messenger, Jesus went to the place where the demons are incarcerated in hell. He didn't go to them to proclaim the gospel for purposes of salvation but rather to make the announcement that He was King of Kings and Lord of Lords, all authority had been given to Him, and He had the keys of hell and death. He went there to tell them that He had defeated Satan, and that He would live forever! Jesus also preached the gospel to those who were in Abraham's bosom, for their salvation. These people had died in faith, waiting for the redemption of the Messiah, just as is described in Hebrews 11:13–16. They were first to receive the good news of the resurrection.

+ **He Was Made Alive in His Body**

12. (a) When Christ rose from the dead, what did He become for those who believe? (1 Corinthians 15:20b)

_____

(b) How is Jesus described in Revelation 1:5?

_____

13. (a) After Jesus was resurrected and taught His disciples about the kingdom for forty days, where did He ascend? Complete the following:

Acts 1:11a: *"This same Jesus, who was taken up from you* _____

_____*...."*

Acts 2:33a: "*Therefore* [Jesus] *being exalted* _____ _____ _____

_____ _____ _____ *….*"

(b) What name has God the Father bestowed upon Jesus? (Philippians 2:9)

_____

14. (a) While we were once dead in trespasses, what are we now? (Ephesians 2:5b)

_____

(b) What is our spiritual position in Christ Jesus? (Verse 6)

_____

When we identify with Jesus' death, burial, and resurrection,
we become a new creation to rule and reign with Him.

Conclusion

Jesus conquered sin, the devil and his demons, death, and hell. Realizing that Jesus triumphed over these foes, which were unconquerable to mankind, is key to understanding His full work of redemption. Christ's resurrection from the dead accomplished the following:

+ Restored us to communion with the spiritual life of God. He made us one with the Father again; we have been reconciled and reunited with Him. (See 2 Corinthians 5:18; 1 John 1:3.)

+ Implanted in our mortal bodies the resurrection life, which will fully manifest when Christ returns for His church, at which point our bodies will be glorified like His. (See Romans 8:11.)

+ Returned us to eternity in the presence of God. This is the consummation of Christ's perfect work on the cross and His resurrection. (See 1 Thessalonians 4:17; Revelation 21:1–3.)

+ Seated us in heavenly places to rule with Christ. After paying for our sins and being raised from the dead, Jesus sat down forever on His throne at the right hand of the

Father as our High Priest. His sitting down symbolized His authority, government, and reign, because His work was finished. Once His atoning work was accomplished, He gave us back the dominion that Adam had lost and—even more remarkable— seated us together with Him in His heavenly rule. The Son of God is the only King who allows His subjects to reign with Him. This is our inheritance! (See, for example, Ephesians 2:5–6; Hebrews 4:14; 6:20; 7:26–28; 10:11–13.)

Prayer of Activation

Lord Jesus, thank You for dying for us, descending into hell, and paying the price for our sins. You received the wrath of God in our place. We give You all honor and glory. From this day forward, we surrender to You, and we ask You to rule over us and to live Your life through us.

We ask You to resurrect our lives, our visions, our dreams, our health, our homes, and our finances. Jesus, we adore You because the impossible has become possible through Your resurrection. We are healed and free. We receive creative miracles, right now! We are able to exercise dominion and rule over the enemy in the territory You have given us. No longer do we need to be dominated and controlled by circumstances, problems, or Satan. Thank You for making us fellow heirs with You of God's blessings. Amen!

Action Steps

+ Offer heartfelt praise to Jesus for dying physically and spiritually and tasting the "second death" on your behalf, so that you could be raised to newness of life in Him. (See Romans 6:4.)

+ Are you living from the perspective of reigning in the heavenly places in Christ Jesus? Reread Ephesians 2:5–6 and commit it to memory in order to awaken your faith to the spiritual reality of your position in Christ.

ENCOUNTERS WITH GOD'S KINGDOM

A Stillborn Baby Is Raised from the Dead in a Morgue

A woman named Amalia, who is a member of a church in Argentina that is under the spiritual covering of King Jesus Ministry, witnessed the power of the resurrection to raise her child from the dead. She'd had an at-risk pregnancy that had caused her to go into labor in her sixth month. The birth was complicated, and the baby girl was stillborn. The doctors held the infant under observation for several hours, but she was finally declared officially dead, and her body was sent to the morgue. When the church heard the news, they began to intercede for the family.

As soon as Amalia was able, she asked to see her daughter's body, but because of the many rules and regulations, twelve hours passed before she received permission. Finally, she and her husband were allowed to go to the morgue. The forensic doctor led them to a small box where the baby's body lay dead. When he opened the box, Amalia and her husband saw that the baby was wrapped in cloth. Amalia removed the cloth and took her daughter's cold hand in hers to say good-bye. Suddenly, they heard a weak sound, and the baby moved. She was alive! The impact of this experience was so great that Amalia was on the verge of fainting. When the forensic doctor saw what was happening, he started to cry. He couldn't get over his shock. The baby had spent twelve hours in the morgue at extremely low temperatures. She was immediately taken to the neonatal unit and given the attention she required. There, the doctors confirmed that her vital signs were normal.

When the director of the hospital heard what had happened, he suspended every doctor and nurse who had attended at the delivery, thinking the baby's parents would file a malpractice suit, because he did not understand how something like this could occur. Finally, everyone had to admit that what had happened had been a miracle of God. The baby girl had been raised from death by the power of the resurrection of Jesus Christ, while she'd been in the morgue lying in the box! The news went out to the media throughout the country and the world. Today, the baby, Luz Milagros, is with her family, growing strong and healthy. Similar miracles can happen in your life, in your family, and in your church as you apply the power of the resurrection to your circumstances.

Study 5

A Revelation of the Resurrection for the Kingdom Here and Now

"That I may know Him and the power of His resurrection...."
—Philippians 3:10

Introduction

Often, when we hear the message of Christ's resurrection preached in churches, it is presented solely from a historical point of view without revelation. Consequently, we do not often witness God's power manifesting among His people. A revelation of the living Christ distinguishes between those who believe in the resurrection for the here and now—the eternal present—and those who believe in it as a historic event. The former are activated and receive Jesus' supernatural power for advancing His kingdom.

Study Questions

Part I: Ten Essential Revelations of the Resurrection

- **Revelation #1: The Resurrection Is Always Revealed by the Holy Spirit in the "Now"**

1. (a) Read John 19:17–18, 34 and John 20:24–28. Then, explain how the disciple Thomas gained a revelation of the reality of Jesus' resurrection. (John 20:27–28)

_____

_____

_____

_____

(b) What did Jesus say about those who never personally saw the resurrected Christ but who still received the revelation of His resurrection? (John 20:29b)

_____

(c) Because Peter had witnessed the living Christ (see Acts 3:15b) and knew there was power in His name (see verse 16a), what did he say and do to the lame man at the temple gate? (Acts 3:6b–7a)

_____

_____

(d) What happened to the lame man as a result? (Verses 7b, 8b)

_____

_____

+ **Revelation #2: Jesus' Resurrection Is the Demonstration of His Love and Power**

2. Because of the Father's love for us, demonstrated through the death and resurrection of His Son Jesus Christ, what are we called? (1 John 3:1a)

_____

+ **Revelation #3: Jesus' Resurrection Is the Foundation and Sustenance of Christianity**

3. Without the resurrection to culminate the work of the cross, there would be no salvation and no resulting personal transformation, since it is resurrection power that activates that work. Because of Christ's resurrection, in what manner should we now *"walk"*? Complete the following:

Romans 6:4b: *"…just as Christ was raised from the dead by the glory of the Father, even so we also should walk in* _____ _____ _____*."*

The resurrection is the only source of power for transforming the heart.

+ **Revelation #4: If Christ Had Not Resurrected, Our Faith and Message Would Be in Vain**

4. What would have been some of the consequences if Jesus had not resurrected? (1 Corinthians 15:14b–15a, 17b–19)

   _____

   _____

   _____

   _____

+ **Revelation #5: The Resurrection Validates and Vindicates Christ as the Son of God**

5. What was Jesus declared to be by the *"Spirit of holiness"*? Complete the following:

   Romans 1:4: "[Jesus was] *declared to be* _____ _____ _____

   _____ _____ _____ *according to the Spirit of*

   holiness, _____ _____ _____ _____

   _____ _____."

+ **Revelation #6: Christ Is the Only One with a Testimony of Being Permanently Raised from the Dead, Both Spiritually and Physically**

6. (a) What did the resurrected Christ say about Himself? (Revelation 1:18a)

   _____

   _____

   (b) Note a significant contrast between the first Adam and Christ, the *"last Adam."* Complete the following:

   1 Corinthians 15:45: "'*The first man Adam* _____ _____

   _____ _____.' *The last Adam* _____

   _____ _____ _____."

♦ **Revelation #7: The Resurrection Established Christ's Kingdom and Destroyed Satan's Kingdom**

7. (a) What titles belong to Jesus? (Revelation 19:16)

_____

(b) By His death and resurrection, what did Jesus do to the evil principalities and powers of Satan's kingdom? (Colossians 2:15)

_____

Every time we preach the resurrection, we remind Satan of his defeat.

♦ **Revelation #8: Christ's Resurrection Won Our Salvation, Redemption, Justification, and Resurrection**

8. (a) What do we have in Christ that enabled us to enter His kingdom? Complete the following:

Colossians 1:13–14: "[God the Father] *has delivered us from the power of darkness and conveyed us into the kingdom of the Son of His love, in whom* _____

_____ _____ _____ _____

_____, _____ _____ _____ _____."

(b) What will God do for us, just as He did for Jesus? (2 Corinthians 4:14a)

_____

(c) In what way will Jesus transform our bodies when He returns to earth? (Philippians 3:21a)

_____

+ **Revelation #9: The Resurrection Gives Us the Right to Rule Over Everything Jesus Conquered**

9. (a) What will those who receive abundance of grace and the gift of righteousness in Christ do? (Romans 5:17b)

_____

(b) Name two signs that Jesus said would follow those who believe. Complete the following:

Mark 16:17a: *"In My name they will _____ _____*

_____.…"

Verse 18b: *"…they will _____ _____ _____ _____*

_____, _____ _____ _____ _____."

+ **Revelation #10: The Message of the Power of the Resurrection Releases Miracles, Signs, and Wonders Here and Now**

10. (a) With what did the apostles give witness to the resurrection of Jesus? (Acts 4:33a)

_____

(b) What happened when Jesus' disciples *"went out and preached everywhere"*? (Mark 16:20b)

_____

When the Holy Spirit reveals the resurrection,
it is confirmed with miracles, signs, and wonders.

Part II: How to Walk in the Power of the Resurrection

+ **Principle #1: Die to the "Old Man"—the Flesh, or the Carnal Self**

11. (a) What did Jesus say about those who desire to follow Him? (Luke 9:23b)

_____

(b) When Jesus was in the garden of Gethsemane, what did He pray, expressing His total submission to God the Father? Complete the following:

Matthew 26:39b: *"Nevertheless, _____ _____ _____ _____,*

_____ _____ _____ _____."

(c) How do we avoid fulfilling the lust of the flesh? (Galatians 5:16a)

_____

REFLECTIONS ON DYING TO THE CARNAL SELF

Jesus said, *"He who loves his life will lose it, and he who hates his life in this world will keep it for eternal life"* (John 12:25). The Greek word translated *"life"* in the first two instances in this verse is *psuche*, which means "the soul" (NASC, G5590), or indicates "the seat of personality."[1] The soul consists of the mind, will, and emotions; it is the center of our feelings, desires, affections, and preferences. I believe that Christ was basically saying that if we love our *psuche*—what we think, feel, and want—without pursuing what God wants, we will die spiritually. But if we hate our lives, in the sense of turning away from *"the spirit of the world"* (1 Corinthians 2:12), we will receive eternal life. We cannot lead selfish lives and the life of the resurrection at the same time; it is impossible for us to manifest both at once. One must die for the other to live. We must die to the old life to make way for our new life in Christ.

We will live to the degree that we are willing to die.

---

1. *Vine's Complete Expository Dictionary of Old and New Testament Words*, 588.

+ **Principle #2: Live by the Faith of Christ Within You, Here and Now**

12. (a) When we have been *"crucified with Christ,"* who lives in us? (Galatians 2:20a)

_____

(b) How do we now live our lives *"in the flesh"*? (Verse 20b)

_____

(c) Since we have been spiritually raised with Christ, what are we to seek? (Colossians 3:1)

_____

(d) What are we to set our minds on, and what aren't we to set our minds on? (Verse 2)

_____

Christ's faith dwelling in us is the resurrection life.

+ **Principle #3: Receive Your Inheritance of the Resurrection by Faith**

13. What are some spiritual truths the apostle Paul particularly wanted the Ephesian believers to know? (Ephesians 1:18b)

_____

_____

---

*If the revelation of the resurrection is absent,
there will be no supernatural power in the church.*

+ **Principle #4: Know Christ in the Power of His Resurrection**

14. (a) What is another spiritual truth Paul wanted the Ephesians to know? (Ephesians 1:19a)

_____

(b) What did Jesus say about Himself? (John 11:25a)

_____

(c) What was one of Christ's mandates for His disciples? Complete the following:

Matthew 10:8: "*Heal the sick, cleanse the lepers,* _____ _____

_____....*"*

KEY DEFINITION: Paul wrote, "*That I may know* [Christ] *and the power of His resurrection, and the fellowship of His sufferings, being conformed to His death*" (Philippians 3:10). The Greek word translated "*know*" in this verse is *ginosko*, which means "to come to know, recognize, perceive" (NASC, G1097). These definitions indicate "to experience."

The resurrection life that flows through us is supernatural by nature and origin. Miracles, signs, wonders, and the raising of the dead should be the norm for us.

+ **Principle #5: Recognize and Understand God's Sovereignty**

15. What is in God's hand? (Job 12:10b)

_____

+ **Principle #6: Receive a Rhema, or a Revealed "Now" Word, from the Holy Spirit**

16. (a) What did Jesus say to the people mourning a young girl who had died, based on revelation knowledge He had received from God? (Luke 8:52b)

_____

(b) The crowd of mourners ridiculed Jesus for what He had said, because they knew the girl was dead. Yet, based on the knowledge He had received, what did Jesus do, and what was the result? (Verses 54–55a)

_____

_____

(c) What revelation knowledge did Jesus receive regarding the outcome of Lazarus' sickness (and subsequent death), as well as its purpose? (John 11:4)

_____

_____

Conclusion

Christ's resurrection proves His deity, His lordship, and His kingdom. Satan is terrified of the testimony of the resurrection because he knows it has the power to overturn the kingdom of darkness. Jesus conquered sin, death, hell, the devil and his demons, sickness, the old nature and the flesh, the world, fear, poverty, vengeance, rejection, curses, and much more. Everything Jesus Christ defeated is now subject to His dominion—it is a conquered enemy.

Through Christ's sacrifice on the cross, we are forgiven; through His resurrection, we begin to operate in His power. The message of the cross and the message of the resurrection must always be proclaimed together. Praise God that Jesus rose from the dead and defeated Satan, taking from him all power and authority!

I encourage you today to take authority and dominion through Christ over every enemy that was conquered by His resurrection. Cast out demons, heal the sick, and raise the dead. Raising the dead is an amazing miracle and sign. Jesus did it, the apostles did it, I have done it, others whom I have taught and trained have done it, and you can do it, too! Release the power of His resurrection!

Prayer of Activation

Holy Spirit, You are the Administrator and Executor of the power of Christ's resurrection. We ask You to enlighten our understanding with the spirit of wisdom and revelation, so we can know the power of the resurrection, apply it to our lives, and release it over others who are in need.

Let Jesus' resurrection life and faith flow through us today. We acknowledge that the power of the resurrection is available and active wherever we go. We can do all things through Christ who strengthens us. Nothing is impossible for us, as nothing is impossible for God. We are an extension of the resurrected Christ on earth in order to advance His kingdom. He lives, and we live according to His life and faith. In the name of Jesus, amen!

Action Steps

- As you have just prayed, receive the revelation by the Holy Spirit right now of the power of Christ's resurrection and start living according to it.

- We must die to the "carnal self" each day. This is a lifelong process. Start today by renouncing any part of your lifestyle that is not yielded to God, and pray to your heavenly Father, "Lord, not my will but Yours be done."

- Ask the Holy Spirit to give you an experience of Christ's resurrection power in every aspect, so that you will know the power of Christ as dominion (territorial power), anointing (the power to serve), faith (the power to do miracles), rule (the power of God in the realm of authority), perseverance (the power for character transformation), strength (the power for spiritual warfare), and prosperity (the power to gain wealth).

- As you receive revelation knowledge from the Holy Spirit regarding various circumstances, and as you act on that revelation in faith, exhibit the proof of Jesus' resurrection through miracles, signs, wonders, and the raising of the dead. Be willing to suffer persecution for proclaiming the complete message of the kingdom, the cross, and Christ's resurrection as you release His supernatural power on the earth.

ENCOUNTERS WITH GOD'S KINGDOM

Resurrection from the Dead After "Mistaken Identity"

Mani Efran is a Turkish pastor and prophet. He and several of the leaders whom he has been training attended a conference in Turkey where Apostle Maldonado taught on the supernatural. All the attendees left filled with supernatural faith to pray for the sick. One of the pastors under the covering of Pastor Efran's church returned to Iran, where a church member asked if he could pray for his father, who was very ill. This pastor and his wife went to the hospital, but when they arrived at the room, the nurses were disconnecting the machines that had been hooked up to the patient, who had just died. As soon as they were alone with the man, however, they laid hands on his dead body, declaring that God would resurrect him. When nothing happened, they were saddened and went to find the man's family in the waiting room.

They offered their condolences and apologized for arriving too late, but the man's son said, "What are you talking about? My father is not dead!" And he ran to check on his father, who was indeed alive—in a different hospital room. In the meantime, another family was shouting with joy, saying that *their* father had awakened from the dead, asking, "Where is the couple that prayed for me? Bring me the couple. I saw them!"

As it turned out, the desk clerk had directed the pastor and his wife to the wrong room. God had raised the other man from the dead after their prayers! This man said that he'd had a vision of his hospital room, and he'd seen his dead body as he'd watched the couple come into the room and pray for him. He recognized them when he saw them again. He was totally healed and started telling everyone that Jesus had resurrected him! Consequently, he and his entire family received Jesus as Savior. Although the man for whom this couple had prayed was not the person they had originally gone to see, God still did the miracle because of their supernatural boldness. They had prayed for his resurrection, and the power of God had raised him from death!

Study 6

THE SPIRITUAL CONFLICT BETWEEN TWO KINGDOMS

"For we do not wrestle against flesh and blood, but against principalities, against powers, against the rulers of the darkness of this age, against spiritual hosts of wickedness in the heavenly places."
—Ephesians 6:12

Introduction

We are living in times of great conflict! Many people are aware of the wars and acts of political unrest that are taking place around the world, but most people overlook the invisible spiritual conflict that takes place daily between the kingdom of light and the kingdom of darkness. Each person on earth, without exception, is aligned with either one kingdom or the other, whether he realizes it or not. There is no neutrality. Simply put, obedience to God and His delegated authority aligns us with the kingdom of God, while disobedience to God aligns us with the kingdom of darkness.

To truly fathom this conflict between the kingdom of God and the kingdom of Satan, we must have a thorough understanding of how these two kingdoms are diametrically opposed to one another. In this study, we will learn how God's kingdom rules and then contrast it with how the kingdom of darkness functions. We will also further examine how Jesus thoroughly defeated Satan through His death and His resurrection.

Study Questions

Part I: How the Kingdom of God Rules

+ **Through Fatherhood**

The kingdom of God is not just a system of laws and statutes, nor is it merely the association between a sovereign and his subjects. It is the relationship of a Father to His children, and vice versa. God is a Father to us in numerous ways. He provides us with identity as His children; He affirms, nourishes, strengthens, and disciplines us for our good; He reveals our purposes and enables us to fulfill them. It is essential for us to relate to God as our Father in order to serve in His kingdom.

1. When we have "seen" Jesus—His love, power, priorities, and so forth—whom have we "seen" at the same time? (John 14:9b)

   _____

2. (a) When we become God's children, what else do we become in relation to Him? Complete the following:

   Romans 8:17: *"If children, then* _____; _____ _____

   _____ *and* _____ _____ _____ _____."

   (b) What is our heavenly Father's ultimate goal for us? Complete the following:

   1 John 3:2: *"...when [God the Father] is revealed,* _____ _____ _____

   _____ _____ *, for we shall see Him as He is."*

+ **Through Revelation, or Revealed Knowledge**

3. Through whom do we receive knowledge from God? (John 14:26a)

   _____

4. (a) After they had ministered to the Lord and fasted, what instruction did the leaders at the church in Antioch receive from the Holy Spirit regarding Saul (Paul) and Barnabas? (Acts 13:2)

   _____

   (b) How did the leaders respond to this instruction? (Verse 3)

   _____

   _____

(c) What revelation did the prophet Agabus receive? (Acts 11:28b)

_____

(d) How did the disciples respond to this message? (Verse 29)

_____

(e) What revelation did Paul receive regarding the man who had been lame since birth? (Acts 14:9b)

_____

(f) What did Paul do based on that revealed knowledge? What happened after that? (Verse 10)

_____

_____

+ **Through People's Voluntary Obedience and Submission**

5. (a) Record some statements that Jesus made, showing that God invites us to enter His kingdom of our own free will and receive its benefits.

Matthew 16:24: _____

_____

Matthew 11:28: _____

_____

John 7:37b: _____

(b) As God instructed the Israelites, what should we do to *"eat the good of the land"*? (Isaiah 1:19)

_____

_____

Being under authority is the key to exercising authority.

Part II: How the Kingdom of Darkness Rules

* **Through People's Spiritual Ignorance**

6. (a) What is one method by which Satan, as the *"god of this age,"* prevents people from believing the gospel and keeps them in spiritual ignorance? (2 Corinthians 4:4a)

_____

(b) What does Satan do when people hear the word of the kingdom but don't understand it? (Matthew 13:19)

_____

The kingdom of darkness and of "religion" thrives on our tendency to continue in spiritual ignorance.

---

* **Through People's Disobedience**

7. What term did Paul use for the people through whom the devil is working to advance his kingdom of darkness? (Ephesians 2:2b)

_____

8. What are some of the works of disobedience? (Colossians 3:5b NIV)

_____

Any religion that is unable to deal with a person's rebellion is ineffective.

<u>KEY DEFINITIONS</u>: Satan is called the *"prince of the power of the air"* (Ephesians 2:2). The Greek word translated *"prince"* is *archon*, which means "one who is first in rank or power," "chief," "magistrate," "prince," or "ruler" (STRONG, NASC G758). The word translated *"power"* is *exousia*, and among its meanings are "authority," "jurisdiction" (STRONG, G1849), and "power to act" (NASC, G1849). From these two Greek words, we can conclude that Satan is a ruling fallen angel; he is the chief of the realm or jurisdiction of the *"air."*

REFLECTIONS ON THE "PRINCE OF THE POWER OF THE AIR"

The word *"air"* in Ephesians 2:2 refers to the atmosphere adjacent to the surface of the earth. When Satan was defeated by Jesus, he had to let go of his dominion of the earth. However, the iniquity of those who are still disconnected from God and who remain under the devil's sway allows him to retain some measure of rule. Satan's kingdom has access to people's lives directly through their own sin and rebellion. It also has the ability to manipulate and tempt people through the avenue of the earth's atmosphere. Even though the atmosphere is not a tangible territory, we can recognize the influence of Satan's dominion there by the transmissions of unhealthy programming, music, and Web content that people distribute over the airwaves through television, radio, and the Internet. The church must take a stand and exercise dominion over the airwaves by broadcasting programs containing God's Word and His principles, in order to dispel this negative atmosphere.

+ **Through Domination and Control**

9. (a) What did Satan inflict on a slave girl in order to dominate and control her? (Acts 16:16a)

_____

(b) How did Paul remove the kingdom of darkness from the girl? (Verse 18b)

_____

_____

10. Paul asked of the believers in the church at Galatia who had *"bewitched"* them (Galatians 3:1), thus dominating them by drawing them away from the true message of the gospel of the kingdom. What error did Paul indicate they had fallen into? Complete the following:

    Galatians 3:3 (NIV): *"After beginning with the Spirit, are you now* _____

    _____ _____ _____ _____ _____

    _____ _____?"*

11. Though it often seems as if our conflicts and problems are caused by other people, what are we ultimately battling against? (Ephesians 6:12b)

    _____

    _____

    _____

The law of the kingdom of darkness is domination and control over people.
The law of the kingdom of God is submission freely offered to Him.

Part III: Four Results of Jesus' Victory Over Satan at the Cross

  ◆ **Satan Was Defeated**

12. Since Christ Jesus has defeated Satan, what has He enabled us to be in the midst of *"tribulation, or distress, or persecution"* (Romans 8:35), or any other adverse situation in life? Complete the following:

    Romans 8:37: *"In all these things we are* _____ _____

    _____ *through Him who loved us."*

◆ Satan Was Dethroned

13. Satan, as the *"strong man,"* maintained the security of his kingdom of darkness for a time. (See Luke 11:21.) However, what did Jesus, the One who was *"stronger than he,"* do to dismantle Satan's kingdom after He invaded his "palace" and overcame him? (Verse 22)

_____

_____

By way of the cross, Jesus inflicted on Satan a total, permanent, eternal, and irrevocable defeat.

◆ Satan Was Disarmed

14. At the same time that Jesus *"disarmed principalities and powers"* (Colossians 2:15), He equipped believers with the *"whole armor of God"* (Ephesians 6:11), among other spiritual resources, so that we could resist the devil's attacks and drive out the kingdom of darkness from the "territories" it has taken. List the pieces of our spiritual armor. (Ephesians 6:14–17 NIV)

_____

_____

◆ Satan Was Destroyed

15. (a) When Jesus destroyed Satan, He also nullified all the enemy's power. What particular power did the writer of Hebrews mention in this regard? (Hebrews 2:14b)

_____

(b) What did Jesus accomplish for human beings, who had been subject to bondage because of a fear of this power? (Verse 15a)

_____

16. What did Jesus say was clear evidence that the kingdom of God had arrived? (Matthew 12:28a)

_____

_____

Casting out demons is a manifestation of the dominion and rule of God's kingdom.

Conclusion

The moment we were born again, we were immediately transferred into God's kingdom of light. At that instant, we entered into spiritual warfare with Satan's kingdom of darkness. When we begin to remove Satan's kingdom from various territories he has taken, he fights for his life. He doesn't want to be forced out of any territory he has gained in people and places. He likes to challenge the authority we have been given in Christ. Therefore, we must stand on our God-given authority and resist him.

Even though we have been delivered from Satan's power, the final sentence against the enemy has yet to be carried out by Christ. While Satan no longer has dominion over us, he will continue trying either to bring us back into his kingdom or to undermine our spiritual effectiveness. Until his final defeat at the end of the age, Satan has still been given the legal right by God to fight against us using three methods—*temptation* (see, for example, Matthew 6:13), *persecution* (see, for example, 2 Timothy 3:12), and *accusation* (see, for example, Revelation 12:10). But we have the power and authority in Christ to overcome him!

For you to present a real threat to the kingdom of darkness, you must be ready to protect yourself from, and resist, satanic attacks. God's kingdom is not about theology or doctrine but about resurrection power that can defeat the enemy. Let's remember that the only authority the devil can have over us is the authority we give him through our disobedience. (See, for example, Ephesians 4:27.) Even though believers cannot be physically possessed by demons, they can still be influenced by them; there may be areas in our lives that are being held captive by Satan due to unforgiveness or generational curses. This is why deliverance is something we must practice regularly. When we are free of sin and are obeying God, the enemy cannot prevail against us. He might have some power, but he no longer has authority, and he cannot defeat us unless we allow it. In the power of Christ's resurrection, we can force Satan to submit, and we can destroy all of his works!

Prayer of Activation

Deliverance will not come if we are passive and do nothing, or if we just cite Scripture. It will come when we take action and rebuke demonic entities in the authority of Jesus' name. I have been ministering for more than two decades, and I have learned to first lead people to carry out certain conditions for their deliverance. This helps them to be free of all demonic oppression operating in their minds, wills, and emotions. To receive deliverance—and to stay free—we must:

+ Have a personal revelation of Jesus as Lord and Savior.

+ Humble ourselves before God (those who refuse to humble themselves should not continue with the deliverance).

+ Confess all sins, whether of commission or omission.

+ Repent wholeheartedly.

+ Choose to forgive everyone who has offended us.

+ Desperately desire our deliverance from the enemy's oppression.

+ Break any pacts we have made with the occult through witchcraft, Santeria, or any other false religion or sect.

+ Believe, confess, and receive, by faith, the divine exchange that took place at the cross of Christ.

+ Exhale, so that every evil spirit can leave our bodies.

We will use the following prayer as a guide. It will keep us from omitting any important aspects of deliverance. Remember that as you pray this prayer, you should exhale, as an act of faith, so that every evil spirit will leave you.

Dear Lord, we believe that You are the Son of God and that You died on the cross for our sins; that You were raised from the dead so we could be forgiven and receive eternal life. Right now, we take hold of Your work and renounce all religious self-righteousness and any other sense of pride that does not come from You. We ask for Your mercy and grace, knowing that we have nothing to boast about. We confess and wholeheartedly repent of all the sins we have committed, as well as everything we should have done but failed to do. We choose to end our sinful lifestyle so that we may have new life in You. Of our own free will, we make a decision to follow You. We forgive everyone who has hurt us and has wished us harm. We renounce and let go of all unforgiveness, bitterness, hatred, and resentment. We specifically forgive [mention the names of those who have hurt you], and we ask for Your supernatural grace to forgive them.

We renounce every pact we have made with the occult, whether through witchcraft, divination, or false doctrines or religions. We also commit ourselves to destroying every object in our homes or offices that is associated with the occult and idolatry.

Lord Jesus, thank You for taking our curse on the cross so we could receive Your blessing. We are redeemed and free in Your name. We stand with You against Satan and his demons. We renounce the curses we have seen in operation in our lives [mention all the generational curses you may have identified: sickness, depression, alcoholism, adultery, suicide, premature death, and anything else]. Now, we receive Your blessings. We resist the devil and submit to You. We order every demon that has control over our lives, health, finances, and family to leave, right now! We cast every demon out, now, in the name of Jesus. We are free!

Action Steps

+ Are you struggling with an issue you cannot identify? Maybe you can tangibly sense the hatred of demons toward you and God. If so, ask the Lord for the discernment to identify and deal with any evil entities that are working against you. Cast them out of your life, your home, your church, your business, and any other place connected to you.

+ Satan will use our carnal nature, or "flesh," in his attempts to defeat us, because the carnal nature is the area in which temptation takes place. However, the flesh is not the same thing as the devil, so we have to deal with it differently than we deal with him. When we accept Jesus, our spirit is born again, but our soul is merely "rescued"—it is now capable of being renewed, but it is not yet fully transformed. From the moment of our salvation, we must continually work on the transformation of our souls. The carnal nature is the combination of our ungodly passions, perverted emotions, bad thoughts, stubbornness, and evil desires. Many believers today seem to be trying to "cast out" the flesh and "crucify" the devil. They have it backward. Jesus defeated the devil and sin at the cross, but it is our responsibility to crucify the flesh; no one else can do this for us. When we crucify the flesh, we submit to the lordship of Jesus Christ and no longer live a sinful lifestyle. We live by the faith of the Son of God. Therefore, submit yourself to God fully, right now, and turn away from any sin you have been holding on to. Do this daily. Then, after you have learned to live in this way, if you still fail to experience spiritual victory in a particular area, you must suspect Satan and his demons as the cause of your problem and rebuke them. Carry out the conditions listed before the "Prayer of Activation," above, and then pray the prayer. Remember, when you order demons to leave, they will not obey you unless you have first crucified your flesh in the area from which you want to expel them—regardless of whether you are expelling them from yourself or another person.

+ Rebuke the enemy, pull down his strongholds, and cast out demons from people in the name of Jesus, as you receive revelation and discernment from the Holy Spirit.

ENCOUNTERS WITH GOD'S KINGDOM

Delivered from Demons After Being Possessed for Thirty Years

Pastor Ellie Davidian is a former devout Shiite Muslim from Iran. She was wonderfully saved through a dream in which Jesus introduced Himself to her. She and her husband started a ministry with a passion to reach the Muslim community. Their congregation consists of Muslims who have emigrated from Iran and who have been saved and delivered. When Pastor Ellie began to watch Apostle Maldonado's TV program, she immediately identified with his teaching about visions and revelations, and the supernatural power of God took her ministry to the next level.

Several weeks after Pastor Ellie received Apostle Maldonado's teachings on supernatural authority, a woman named Suzanne, who was listening to Pastor Ellie's radio program in Iran, was radically saved. A couple of weeks later, Suzanne visited her aunt and cousin Elizabeth, who had been violently demon-possessed for the past thirty years. Elizabeth had lost her own mother to breast cancer when she was five years old, and her two sisters had died of breast cancer, also, so her aunt had raised her.

People could hardly get near Elizabeth because she was so aggressive. For example, when someone tried to feed her an orange, she would snatch it out of the person's hand, screaming, and bite into it immediately without even peeling it. Her aunt testified that Elizabeth would tear apart all her own clothing, bedding, and pillows. She could not stand to wear a single piece of clothing, so she would cover herself only with blankets. She also had been urinating on herself for the past twenty-five years, so that the smell penetrated the walls. When Suzanne visited her aunt, she found her cousin with a chain fastened around her stomach; the chain was attached to a hole in the wall, to keep her from harming others. The atmosphere there was charged with spiritual opposition.

Suzanne was able to contact Pastor Ellie via cell phone, and, through it, Pastor Ellie preached to Elizabeth, who began screaming. Pastor Ellie commanded the demons—spirits of fear and suicide—to leave her, in the name of Jesus. Suddenly, Elizabeth stopped screaming. Pastor Ellie then told Suzanne, "You have the authority, in the name of Jesus, to continue praying." So, Suzanne began to pray, sing, and worship God, and Elizabeth calmed down.

After this, for the first time in thirty years, the ropes and chains were removed from Elizabeth, and she began to behave normally. That night, she showered for the first time in two-and-a-half decades. She ate her dinner calmly like everyone else, and she slept on a bed with her clothes on. The aunt felt such relief and thankfulness to Jesus over the deliverance of her niece that she cried and confessed Jesus as her Savior! Pastor Ellie had discovered that she had authority through Jesus to cast out demons from people who are possessed, and she began to manifest Jesus' power in her territory!

Study 7

THE GOSPEL OF THE KINGDOM PROCLAIMED IN THE NOW

"And they went out and preached everywhere, the Lord working with them and confirming the word through the accompanying signs."
—Mark 16:20

Introduction

What message did Jesus preach as He went about His earthly ministry? He preached *"the **gospel of the kingdom**"*; in accordance, He healed *"all kinds of sickness and all kinds of disease among the people"* (Matthew 4:23).

The Greek word translated *"gospel"* is *euaggelion*, which means "a good message" (STRONG, G2098), or "good tidings" (NASC, G2098). It is the good news! Jesus brought the good news, but it was specific news. It was the good news of the kingdom. If we leave out the kingdom, we are not proclaiming the same gospel that Jesus announced. The kingdom gospel we proclaim must be aligned with what God is revealing today, not just with what He has revealed in the past. The gospel of the kingdom is what Jesus is doing through individual believers, and through churches and ministries, in the now.

We cannot proclaim the gospel of the "here and now" without present revelation from God. Some revelation is given for the manifestation of a healing or deliverance. Other revelation enables us to have a deeper encounter with God. What we must realize is that spiritual revelation from our heavenly Father cannot manifest in the physical world without the assistance of human beings, because that is how God designed it to work.

Study Questions

Part I: The True Gospel of the Kingdom Is One of Power and Revelation

1. What power does the gospel have? (Romans 1:16b)

2. (a) What did the apostle Paul marvel over regarding the Galatians' faith? Complete the following:

Galatians 1:6: *"I marvel* _____ _____ _____

_____ _____ _____ _____ *from Him*

who called you in the grace of Christ, _____ _____ _____

_____."

(b) What is the essence of the true gospel of the kingdom, through which God's power is activated? Complete the following:

Galatians 2:16a: *"...a man is not justified by the works of the law but by* _____

_____ _____ _____."

The power of God does not rest in a personality but in the Truth, which is the Word of God.

REFLECTIONS ON SUBSTITUTE GOSPELS

In today's church, there are various kinds of "gospels" with which the gospel of the kingdom has been replaced, resulting in diluted or abridged human versions devoid of power. Let us review the most common substitute gospels. The *historical gospel*: A belief in a God of history but not in a God who is with us today and will act powerfully on our behalf. The *"future" gospel*: A "gospel" that proclaims forgiveness of sin so a person can go to heaven when he dies but says nothing of reigning with Christ on earth now with dominion authority and power. The *social gospel*: An emphasis on relieving societal problems, such as hunger, poverty, and injustice, but without seeking or relying on God's supernatural power, through which people can be healed physically, emotionally, and mentally, and through which they have access to God's abundant provision, power, and strength. The *gospel of conformity*: A "gospel" that does not address the root of human rebellion against God nor challenge people to change, so that they are left in sickness, scarcity, and oppression and in a spiritually stagnant condition, unable to move forward, retaining their sin and never regaining their dominion. The *motivational gospel*: A "self-help" message in which God's Word is spoken without power, the cross and the resurrection of Jesus are not proclaimed, and the supernatural is absent. It is a gospel adapted to what people want to hear, and it fails to confront them with the destructiveness of their sin, in an effort to avoid offending them. Churches and ministries that don't preach the gospel of the kingdom produce a complacent Christianity. This is precisely why we don't often see the manifestations of God's power in the church.

The main feature distinguishing the gospel of the kingdom from false and incomplete "gospels" is supernatural evidence of God's presence and power.

---

3. (a) In the days of Samuel the prophet, the Israelites were being led astray by the sons of Eli the high priest. (See 1 Samuel 2:22–24.) What was a sign of the spiritual drought in Israel? (1 Samuel 3:1b)

    _____

    (b) Where there is no revelation from God, what occurs? (Proverbs 29:18a)

    _____

<u>KEY DEFINITION</u>: In the New Testament, the word "*revelation*" is translated from the Greek word *apokalupsis*. It means "disclosure" and has connotations of "appearing," "coming," "lighten," "manifestation," "be revealed," and "revelation" (STRONG, G602); it also means "an uncovering" (NASC, G602). The verb form, *apokalupto*, signifies "to disclose," "to reveal" (STRONG, G601), or "to uncover" (NASC, G601). A revelation from God is something that was previously unknown to the person receiving it. It always brings new knowledge or insight to light or manifests something fresh.

Revelation is a fragment of the knowledge of God that comes into our spirit in an instant, without the need for prior research or investigation, according to God's will and timing.

---

4. Among the five "ministry gifts" given to the church by Christ, which gifts are particularly able to bring fresh revelation from God to His people? Complete the following:

Ephesians 4:11: *"And [Christ] Himself gave some to be* _____,

some _____, *some evangelists, and some pastors and teachers…."*

Every move of God begins with a divine revelation.

Part II: Revelation Must Be Acted Upon

5. (a) What revelation did the woman who suffered from the continual flow of blood express regarding her healing? (Mark 5:28)

   _____

   (b) What action did the woman take based on this revelation? (Verse 27)

   _____

   (c) What happened next, and what did Jesus tell her? (Verses 29, 34)

   _____

   _____

6. (a) What revelation of Jesus' authority and power did the centurion explain as the reason Jesus did not have to go to his servant in order to heal him of his paralysis? (Matthew 8:8b–9)

   _____

   _____

   _____

   _____

(b) What statement did Jesus make about the centurion's faith? (Matthew 8:10)

_____

(c) Due to the centurion's revelation knowledge and faith, what happened to the centurion's servant? (Verse 13b)

_____

Each time God reveals a truth, we are activated to obey it and "own" it.

Part III: Stewards of God's Revelation

7. (a) How did Paul receive the gospel that he preached? (Galatians 1:11–12)

_____

(b) The revelation of the mystery of Christ—His coming to earth to die for our sins and be resurrected—had been kept secret by God since the world began. What did Paul say had occurred concerning this mystery? Complete the following:

Romans 16:25b–26a: "…*kept secret since the world began but* _____ _____

_____ _____ _____."

(c) How did Paul refer to the message of the gospel that he proclaimed? Complete the following:

Romans 16:25a: "*Now to Him who is able to establish you according to* _____

_____ *and the preaching of Jesus Christ.…*"

---

*"Our" gospel of the kingdom is our personal experience of
what God has done and is doing in our lives.*

(d) In addition to direct revelation from God, on what should the establishment of our faith be based? Complete the following:

Romans 16:26: "…*by* _____ _____

_____ *has been made known to all nations, according to the commandment of the everlasting God, for obedience to the faith.*"

8. Whenever we receive a revelation or a manifestation of God's power, we become its caretaker, or steward. What is required of a steward? (1 Corinthians 4:2)

_____

To preach is to proclaim the truth of God's Word. To testify is to share personal knowledge as a result of experiencing His Word and power.

Part IV: Preaching the Gospel with Supernatural Evidence in the Now

9. (a) What did Jesus say would be a major sign of His return and the end of the age? (Matthew 24:14a)

_____

(b) For what reason would the gospel be preached? (Verse 14b)

_____

10. After John the Baptist was imprisoned by Herod, he sent two of his disciples to ask Jesus if He was truly the Messiah. (See Matthew 11:2–3.) What did Jesus say to confirm that He was the Messiah? (Verse 5)

_____

_____

_____

Where there is no supernatural proof, or evidence, there is no kingdom, only abstract theology.

---

11. With what did God bear witness through the apostles that the message of salvation through Christ was true? (Hebrews 2:4)

_____

12. (a) In what two ways did Paul say Christ had worked through him to accomplish the spreading of the gospel? (Romans 15:18b NIV)

_____

(b) What supernatural manifestations were demonstrated in Paul's ministry, and through whose power did they come? (Verse 19a NIV)

_____

(c) What did Paul say he had accomplished through what he had both said and done? Complete the following:

Romans 15:19b (NIV): "I have _____ _____ _____

_____ _____ _____." "

The gospel of the kingdom can never be separated from saving souls,
healing bodies, and casting out demons.

Part V: Principles of Our Kingdom Commission

* **Principle #1: We Are Empowered to Go and Proclaim the Gospel of the Kingdom Now**

13. (a) What commission did Jesus give to His followers? (Matthew 28:19–20a)

_____

_____

_____

(b) What is the first word of Matthew 28:19?

_____

(c) Recall what happened when the apostles *"went out and preached everywhere"* (Mark 16:20a). (Verse 20b)

_____

Supernatural signs and evidence are guaranteed to those who "go."

+ **Principle #2: The Harvest Is Ready Now**

14. (a) Jesus told His disciples that the spiritual *"fields"* of souls were *"already white for harvest"* (John 4:35). What did He say about the condition of the harvest and about the state of the workers? (Luke 10:2a NIV)

_____

(b) For what did Jesus say we should pray? (Verse 2a NIV)

_____

(c) What is God's will for the people of the world? (2 Peter 3:9b)

_____

God's greatest passion is to see everyone in the world—now more than seven billion people—saved, filled with the Holy Spirit, and living holy lives.

+ **Principle #3: We Are to Go and Evangelize Our Own "Ethnos"—and Beyond!**

15. (a) To whom did the disciple Andrew first go to announce that he had found the Messiah (Jesus)? (John 1:41)

_____

(b) What did Andrew do next? (John 1:42)

_____

KEY DEFINITION: The word *"nations"* in Matthew 28:19—*"Go therefore and make disciples of all the nations"*—is translated from the Greek word *ethnos*, from which the English word *ethnic* is derived. *Ethnos* means "a race (as of the same habit), i.e., tribe," with the implication of "nation" or "people" (STRONG, G1484).

REFLECTIONS ON GOING TO OUR "ETHNOS"

People who belong to a particular ethnic group, or *ethnos*, generally speak the same language and have the same beliefs, ways of thinking, values, and traditions, among other shared characteristics. Likewise, one key to developing a nation (*ethnos*) is culture—people coming together who have common standards, customs, and practices. Within nations, there are also subgroups of people, based on their interests, needs, and/or vocations. Each one of these subgroups can be considered an "ethnos," as well. Some of these ethnos subgroups are: politics and government, religion, the media, business, education, science, technology, medicine, economics, sports, entertainment and the arts, and law and justice.

Again, each ethnos has its own mind-set and "language," or terminology. We must identify in which ethnos we participate, so that, together, as the church, we can bring the gospel to all the ethnos of the world. We must start out where we are, in our "Jerusalem and Judea"—our own families, communities, and places of employment—and expand from there. (See Acts 1:8.)

Yet this is not all the church is called to do. I believe that in these last days, evangelism will be accelerated by God's supernatural power, so that believers will be able to cross from one ethnos to another and reach even more people for Christ. Jesus is our best role model for accomplishing this purpose. He interacted with people of various social strata and backgrounds, such as religious leaders, tax collectors, prostitutes, doctors, businesspeople, and Roman centurions. He brought the visible and tangible demonstration of God's power to the rich and the poor; to Jews and Gentiles; to men, women, young people, and children. Today's church needs to be versatile, to let go of its limitations, and to extend outward in the Spirit. I believe the church must become multiracial and multicultural, bringing together different ethnos. The kingdom of God is not about a specific race, nationality, or culture. It includes all races, tribes, nations, and ethnicities.

16. (a) When the apostle Paul, who was Jewish, and his companions arrived in a city to preach the gospel, where did they often go to begin to evangelize? (Acts 9:20; 13:5, 14:1; 17:10; 19:8)

_____

(b) Paul did not evangelize only his own Jewish ethnos. To what groups had God called him to proclaim the gospel, a calling that was fulfilled in his life? (Verse 15)

_____

(c) Paul's ministry in Corinth gives us an example of the manifestation of his calling. Identify some who were converted in that city. (Acts 18:8)

_____

Evangelization in the twenty-first century demands that Christians be able to cross over from one ethnos to another through the supernatural.

Conclusion

The gospel of the kingdom contains great power. It is the power of God for salvation—in all its manifestations of redemption, healing, and deliverance. Jesus came to redeem us from sin, to cure the sick, to deliver the captives, to heal the brokenhearted, and to bring prosperity to the poor. We must let everyone know that the kingdom is among us, here and now!

God's supernatural power will enable us to reach the entire world with the gospel. Yet, it will be impossible for us to carry out our mission if we don't minister where people can be found. You don't have to wait for your pastor to lay hands on you, anoint you, and send you out as a missionary before you can testify of Jesus. You can testify of Him today, in your everyday life—while you are working at the office, eating at a restaurant, attending a sporting event, shopping at a mall, sitting in a theater, or enjoying a vacation—everywhere you go.

God seeks committed and passionate workers who will take His kingdom message into their own ethnos and beyond. The harvest is ready, but the workers are few. Will you begin to proclaim the gospel and testify of what Jesus has done for you? God is calling you to decide, right now! When you do—and as you go—the Lord will confirm His Word through you with signs, miracles, and wonders.

Prayer of Activation

Heavenly Father, we ask You to pour out Your power upon us right now. Activate us and give us a passion for souls as we reach out to people in our own ethnos and beyond, so we can bring them salvation and deliverance. As we go, confirm the gospel of Your kingdom with signs, miracles, and wonders! In Jesus' name, amen.

Action Steps

* "Your" gospel of the kingdom is your personal experience of what God has done and is doing in your life. No one can share what God is doing in you, day by day, like you can, because you live it firsthand. Think about how Jesus has saved you, healed your body, transformed your mind, restored your family, supplied financial provision, brought you peace, joy, and righteousness, and so forth. Testify of God's works in your life to someone every day!

* Have you been living according to the gospel of the "here and now," or have you been living according to the historical gospel, the future gospel, the social gospel, the conformity gospel, or the motivational gospel? Are you producing supernatural evidence that proves Jesus is alive today? Are the sick being healed? Are souls being saved? Are people being delivered of mental and emotional affliction and oppression? Ask the Holy Spirit to search your heart and reveal the answers to these questions. If you have been living an incomplete or substitute gospel, ask God to forgive you through Christ. Then, accept the challenge of living out the true gospel of the kingdom. Rely on the Word of God and the Holy Spirit as you manifest the message of Christ's resurrection in powerful ways, bringing salvation, healing, and deliverance.

ENCOUNTERS WITH GOD'S KINGDOM

A Restored Life Through "Ethnos" Witnessing

Octavio Fernandez was born in the Dominican Republic and was a Major League Baseball player for eighteen years. He says, "My achievements include four times as an American League Gold Glove Winner, a World Series Championship, and five times as an All Star. Although I was brought up by godly parents, I would say they were also very religious. My brothers and I could not engage in activities such as sports or going to the movies, because everything was 'sinful.' I wanted to serve Christ, but I also wanted to enjoy my teenage years, especially playing sports. So, I prayed that God would bless me with a baseball career, and I promised Him I would in turn bless His people and my parents. I became a star at an early age and wanted to enjoy life. Meanwhile, my parents were constantly praying for me. Despite all the success, to my surprise, my heart was empty. In time, I injured my hand severely and had to stop playing. That was devastating to me! The Lord touched one of my teammates to preach to me. But my hand healed, and I returned to the game, did very well, and put God on hold. Everyone, except for my manager, was amazed at how well I was playing. That hurt my feelings, because I wanted his approval, also. There was a void in my heart, and baseball was not my main passion anymore. I needed something real, something better.

"Then, my friend took me to the baseball chapel, where I gave my heart to Jesus. I do not know how to explain it, but I felt that a heavy burden had been lifted from my soul, and I immediately wanted to share the joy I was feeling inside of me. The hatred, hard feelings, resentment, bitterness, and more began to go away. I am so thankful to my teammate. God used him to get to me. Before, I'd always wanted to be perfect in every game; if I did not perform up to that standard, I would get mad at myself, and people misunderstood me. Afterward, I became more tolerant of myself. The biggest transformation took place after I joined King Jesus Ministry. My marriage and family relationships were in 'intensive care,' and the enemy was about to destroy us completely! So, I cried out to God for help, praying early in the morning, as our spiritual fathers teach us. I can definitely say that inner healing has taken place and restoration has begun in every aspect of our lives. Family, ministry, friendship…all has been restored! Today, trivial things don't bother me anymore. My confidence level, founded in my new identity, is much higher than before! Now I can say I am a new creation in Christ Jesus!"

Study 8

THE RESTORATION OF THE SUPERNATURAL IN THE CHURCH

"He who believes in Me, the works that I do he will do also; and greater works than these he will do, because I go to My Father."
—John 14:12

Introduction

The church was birthed in the supernatural, through Jesus' resurrection and the power of the Holy Spirit poured out at Pentecost. Miracles, signs, and wonders established and verified the church's teaching and doctrine. Christians in the New Testament lived a supernatural lifestyle, and the power of the kingdom caused the early church to multiply. Today, the church seems to have lost its life and power, but God has begun to restore the supernatural to individual believers, churches, and ministries who have opened their hearts to receive it. His desire is to fill His entire church with His presence and power.

The gospel of the kingdom is supernatural because it brings heaven to earth. If we are to proclaim this gospel in its fullness, as we discussed in the previous study, we must have an understanding of the supernatural, so we may recognize it and walk in it.

Study Questions

Part I: Principles of the Supernatural
+ **Principle #1: The Supernatural Is the Nature of God Himself**

1. (a) To review, what is God's essential nature? (John 4:24a)

_____

(b) God doesn't depend on the natural realm of time, space, and matter in order to exist, nor does He need anyone or anything else to sustain Him. He has life in and of Himself, and He is the Creator of all things. What did God say when He revealed Himself to Moses, a statement by which we can understand that He lives in the eternal "now"? (Exodus 3:14a)

_____

(c) What are some other ways that God describes Himself? Complete the following:

Revelation 1:8: *"I am the Alpha and the Omega, _____ _____*

_____ _____ _____," says the Lord, *"who is and who was and who is to*

come, _____ _____."

KEY DEFINITION: The Greek word translated as *"Almighty"* in Revelation 1:8 is *pantokrator*, which means "the all-ruling, that is, God as absolute and universal sovereign" (STRONG, G3841), "almighty" (NASC, G3841), or "ruler of all" (VINE, G3841).

(d) Some believers treat God the Father as if He has the same mind-set and finite abilities as fallen human beings. What are some statements that the Scriptures make about this perspective? (Numbers 23:19)

_____

_____

_____

_____

The supernatural, or spiritual, is the form in which God exists.

KEY DEFINITION: *Supernatural* is derived from the prefix *super-*, which means "over" or "above," and the noun *nature.* Therefore, to live in the supernatural means to live above, beyond, or outside of the natural realm. Although the word *supernatural* doesn't appear in the Bible, the concept is demonstrated throughout the Scriptures in the miracles, signs, and wonders that God enacted, which reflect who He is and what He is able to do. Biblical terms and phrases such as "spiritual," "kingdom of heaven," "kingdom of God," "not of this world," and "omnipotent" all refer to our supernatural God and His supernatural realm.

+   **Principle #2: The Supernatural Rules Over the Natural**

2. (a) What did Paul write about the omnipotence of Jesus Christ, through whom, and for whom, all things were created, *"things in heaven and on earth, visible and invisible"* (Colossians 1:16 NIV)? (Verse 17 NIV)

    _____

    (b) By what does God the Son (Jesus Christ) uphold all things? (Hebrews 1:3a)

    _____

The supernatural is the impact and influence of the spiritual world on the physical creation, and its interaction with the same.

---

3. (a) Name some ways in which God rules over the natural world, as well as influences and interacts with people. (Daniel 2:21–22a)

    _____

    _____

    _____

    (b) What did Paul tell the Athenians that God grants us? (Acts 17:25b)

    _____

    (c) What has God determined for the nations of the world? (Verse 26b)

    _____

(d) For what reason has He done the above? (Acts 17:27 NIV)

_____

    ✦ **Principle #3: The Supernatural Is Reality, Not Idolatry, Magic, or Superstition**

4. What did Paul tell the Athenians that God's nature should not be compared to? (Acts 17:29b)

_____

5. (a) Read Acts 8:5–24. At what was Simon, the former sorcerer, amazed? (Verse 13b)

_____

(b) When Simon saw that the Holy Spirit was given to believers through the laying on of the apostles' hands, what did he do and say? (Verses 18b–19)

_____

(c) Why did Peter denounce Simon's request? (Verse 20b)

_____

(d) What did Peter perceive was the reason Simon had a false and sinful attitude toward God's supernatural power? (Verse 23)

_____

═══

The supernatural is truth revealed in the physical dimension.
If the truth is removed, God is, in essence, also removed, leaving only an illusion.

═══

    ✦ **Principle #4: The Supernatural Is Without Limitation**

6. To what degree did God give the Holy Spirit to Jesus—the same degree that is available to believers through Him? (John 3:34b NIV)

_____

7. How long will God's reign last? (Revelation 11:15b)

_____

God's miracles supersede natural facts, reason, logic, and time.

+ **Principle #5: The Supernatural Will Increasingly Manifest on the Earth**

8. (a) What did Jesus say He would do for the person who loved Him and demonstrated that love by keeping His commandments? Complete the following:

   John 14:21b: *"I will _____ _____ and _____*

   _____ _____ _____."*

   (b) What did Jesus say we would do as a result of believing in Him? (John 14:12)

   _____

Where Jesus' ministry on earth ended, the church's life and ministry began.

---

9. (a) How did Peter describe the supernatural manifestations associated with the last days when he quoted an Old Testament prophecy given through Joel? (Acts 2:18–20)

   _____

   _____

   _____

   (b) How are we to respond to supernatural signs of the end times? (Mark 13:7a)

   _____

   (c) What gift from Jesus enables His followers to respond in the above way?
   (John 14:27a)

   _____

Part II: Opposition to the Supernatural

One of the terms for Satan is *"adversary"* (1 Peter 5:8). He opposes God and His purposes in both direct and subtle ways. One of his strategies is to tempt and attack the church so that it will ignore or reject the supernatural, reducing itself to be merely a natural institution. Let us look at two avenues through which he does this.

◆ Through the Spirit of Antichrist

10. (a) What are some truths that the spirit of antichrist denies? (1 John 2:22; 1 John 4:3a)

_____

_____

(b) John wrote of *"many antichrists"* who operated from within the church but then *"went out"* from it. (See 1 John 2:18–19.) What protects us from the spirit of antichrist, so that we remain in the truth? (1 John 2:20)

_____

(c) These *"many antichrists"* had the same characteristic as other people who resisted the truth, whom Paul mentioned. How did Paul describe them? (2 Timothy 3:5a)

_____

KEY DEFINITION: The Greek word for "Christ" is *Christos*, which means "anointed"; it designates the Messiah (STRONG, G5547). The prefix *anti-* in *antichrist* means "against." The enemy's ultimate goal is to replace the true Christ with a false one in people's lives. If he is unable to enter the church through the front door, then he will bring forth people with an antichrist spirit or substitutes for Christ through the back door. The true Christ is the Anointed One who has the supernatural power of the Holy Spirit. (See Luke 4:18–19.) We cannot separate Christ from the anointing, or power, He received from God; if He had lacked this anointing, He would have been a false Messiah. Similarly, "the anointing" is a term we use to refer to the revelation and power a believer receives from God in the Holy Spirit.

Religion is a form or appearance of godliness, without power.

♦ **Through the Greek Mind-set**

The "Greek mind-set" is a perspective based solely on human reason and logic, excluding faith and the supernatural.

11. (a) What did Paul say to warn the Colossians against the Greek mind-set? (Colossians 2:8)

_____

_____

_____

(b) What has God made the wisdom of this world to be? (1 Corinthians 1:20b)

_____

(c) What is Christ to those who are called by God? (Verse 24b)

_____

(d) How can we dismantle the remnants of the Greek mind-set that still influence our thoughts and actions? (2 Corinthians 10:5)

_____

_____

The impossible is founded on reason and established by logic.

Part III: Why We Need the Supernatural

♦ **The Supernatural Manifests Evidence of God's Existence and Reveals Him in the "Now"**

12. (a) Similar to the scriptural pattern we have noted in earlier lessons in this Bible study, when Jesus sent out His twelve disciples to preach the kingdom, what

corresponding evidence of God's immediate presence and power did He enable them to manifest? (Luke 9:1b)

_____

(b) What actions did the disciples subsequently take? (Verse 6)

_____

(c) The apostle Peter raised from the dead a woman named Dorcas, who was a faithful believer, thereby revealing God's resurrection power in the "now." When the people in Dorcas's community of Joppa learned what had happened, how did they respond? (Acts 9:42b)

_____

+ **The Supernatural Establishes the Flow of God's Life in Us**

13. (a) How can we maintain the flow of Jesus' life in us so that we can bear supernatural fruit for God? (John 15:5b)

_____

(b) What did the apostle John pray for the believers to whom he wrote his third epistle? (3 John 1:2)

_____

===

When a believer becomes spiritually stagnant,
it is because the supernatural has stopped flowing through him.

===

+ **The Supernatural Brings Acceleration**

14. (a) What images related to harvesting did God use to describe the blessings and fruitfulness He would bring to His people? (Amos 9:13a)

_____

(b) The early church started with 120 of Jesus' followers. How many believers were added to the church on the day of Pentecost when the gospel was proclaimed in conjunction with the outpouring of the Spirit and supernatural signs? (Acts 2:41)

_____

(c) What was the total number of men who believed after Peter and John healed a man who had been lame from birth, and after Peter preached to the crowd that gathered, proclaiming that Jesus had been raised from the dead? (Acts 4:4)

_____

(d) As the apostles did many signs and wonders among the people, and as the church functioned in unity, how many men and women were *"increasingly added to the Lord"*? (Acts 5:14b)

_____

+ **The Supernatural Overcomes the Impossible**

15. (a) Contrast the natural inability of human beings to save themselves with the supernatural ability of God to save them. Complete the following:

Mark 10:27: *"With men it is impossible, but not with God; for with God* _____

_____ _____ _____.*"*

(b) After Lazarus died, Jesus commanded that the stone sealing his tomb be taken away. Lazarus's sister Martha said, *"Lord, by this time there is a stench, for he has been dead four days"* (John 11:39). What was Jesus' reply? (Verse 40)

_____

When the supernatural is present, spiritual fruit is not only possible but inevitable.

+ **The Supernatural Enables Us to Live Victoriously in Our Times**

16. (a) Who is able to overcome the world? (1 John 5:4a, 5)

_____

(b) What is the victory that has overcome the world? (1 John 5:4b)

_____

_____

(c) What statement did Paul make about living victoriously in the midst of the changing circumstances of life? (Philippians 4:13)

_____

_____

Conclusion

God is restoring *"all things"* to the church, including the supernatural, in preparation for the crowning restoration that will arrive with the second coming of Jesus. (See Acts 3:21.) There are some key words from Acts 3:19–21 that will help us to enter into God's restoration plans. First, what is required if we are to experience restoration? *"**Repent** therefore and be converted, that your sins may be blotted out..."* (Acts 3:19). Next, what will we receive as a result of our repentance? *"...So that times of **refreshing** may come from the presence of the Lord"* (verse 19).

Spiritual refreshing comes through the Holy Spirit and manifests as revivals, the outpouring of the Spirit, the supernatural fire of God, the *shekinah* (the visible manifestation of God's glory), joy, laughter, and other spiritual phenomena. When they receive refreshing, however, many people consider it an end in itself; they enjoy it, but they do not share the power and presence of God they have experienced. For example, they do not minister to other people what they have received from His anointing and glory. Yet spiritual refreshing is a step toward the final objective—extending the kingdom of God in the world and bringing the message of salvation to every person on earth.

That is why each of us must make the decision to expand God's supernatural kingdom. Let us therefore...

+ Recognize God Almighty as a supernatural Being who surpasses reason and the natural world.

+ Renounce the influences exerted by the spirit of antichrist and our culture's overemphasis on the Greek mind-set.

+ Repent of having allowed substitutes for the supernatural to reign in our lives, families, and ministries.

+ Acknowledge our need for the supernatural and ask God to fill us with His presence and power.

+ Commit to walk in the supernatural—not as an isolated event but as a lifestyle.

Together, as the church, let us proclaim the gospel of the kingdom, heal the sick, deliver the captives, raise the dead, and manifest the various gifts of the Holy Spirit, thereby demonstrating the real and living Christ to the world!

Prayer of Activation

Heavenly Father, Your Son Jesus pioneered the restoration of the supernatural on earth. We ask You now to activate us, as the members of His body, to be the pioneers who will continue His supernatural ministry in this world. Empower us to conquer impossibilities—to do the "greater works" that Jesus said we would do because He was returning to You, Father. Do signs and wonders through us as evidence of Your existence, and as revelations of Your presence and power in the here and now, so that multitudes of men and women will be added to Your kingdom. In Jesus' name, amen!

Action Steps

+ The supernatural will not work in our lives if we are not living in obedience to God. For example, we may believe that Jesus has healed us, yet, at the same time, we may be harboring unforgiveness toward someone. (See, for example, Matthew 6:14–15.) If your mind-set and behavior are contrary to God's ways, even in one area of your life, you must repent and receive His forgiveness. Then, continue to seek Him, asking Him to manifest His supernatural power in and through you.

+ Learn to flow in the supernatural by following these steps: (1) Ask God for a breakthrough in the natural realm. A breakthrough occurs when we receive a revelation from Him or when we witness or experience a visible demonstration of His kingdom and power. Therefore, begin to *walk by faith, not by sight* (2 Corinthians 5:7). Ask God to pour out His Spirit in your life and give you breakthroughs. (2) Expect the supernatural. Read Acts 3:1–8, taking special note of verse 5 and the results of the lame man's expectation—which were more than he asked for! (3) Respond to the supernatural. Each time God manifests or reveals a part of His knowledge or wisdom, it is our responsibility to respond to Him. We must release our faith in His presence to capture the supernatural. (See Hebrews 11:6.) In what area is your impossibility? Is it finances, health, or a family relationship? Believe that the supernatural invades your situation, right now, and receive the power of God. (4) Continually reach out to God through prayer and fasting. Revelation and power come from seeking God and being one with Him in the Spirit. (See Colossians 4:2; Matthew 17:14–21.) (5) Seek progressive revelation. Without continual, progressive revelation from God, we cannot function in the spiritual realm or manifest His kingdom on earth, because His kingdom is supernatural in every way. Progressive revelation from God takes us *"from glory to glory."* (See 2 Corinthians 3:18.)

ENCOUNTERS WITH GOD'S KINGDOM

A Miracle of Financial Provision

Not long ago, one of the doctors in our congregation, Dr. Gamal, was experiencing a difficult financial situation because his wife had just lost her job, and he and his wife had also recently had a new baby. Even though they were in a financial crunch, he took a step of faith and decided to accompany me on a mission trip to South America, where we held a conference on the supernatural. He paid all of his expenses with much effort, but he trusted in God's provision. During the trip, we witnessed amazing miracles, but Dr. Gamal was especially impacted when he saw that money began to supernaturally appear in people's wallets and purses. This was a manifestation of the outpouring of the Holy Spirit for supernatural provision.

Dr. Gamal then stood in agreement with his wife, who was watching the conference from Miami via our ministry's Web site, and together they began to declare that if this type of miracle was taking place there, it could happen to them, as well. The week Dr. Gamal returned to Miami, he asked his wife to bring him all the savings they had, because some bills needed to be paid. As she went to get the money box, he was in the living room, praying, "Lord, You promised that I would live in abundance!" When his wife opened the small box that contained their savings, she was astonished to see the amount of cash it contained. She took out the bills and began to count them, and, as she kept counting, she gave a shout that filled the house. When she returned to the living room with the box and the money in hand, she asked her husband how much cash had been left after he'd taken out the money needed for the trip. After he told her it was $1,200, she said, "There is $11,200!" This was a difference of $10,000, which the Lord had supernaturally supplied. Dr. Gamal recalled, "We both jumped for joy, praising God for such a spectacular miracle." For him and his family, the sacrifice of investing in the mission trip, using everything they had and depending totally on God, was worth it. The manifest presence of God produced a miracle in their finances!

Study 9

A Dominion of Kings and Priests

"You are a chosen generation, a royal priesthood, a holy nation,
His own special people, that you may proclaim the praises of Him who called you out of
darkness into His marvelous light."
—1 Peter 2:9

Introduction

As citizens of God's kingdom, we are not just residents of His realm—we are kings and priests under the authority of Christ, our King and High Priest. (See Revelation 1:5–6; 5:9–10.) Our twofold role delineates our God-given dominion on earth. God has always intended for His people to develop a close, intimate relationship with Him while carrying out their purpose as His chosen instruments of kingdom expansion in the world. In this study, we will discover how God wants us to fulfill our ministries of king and priest in the here and now.

Study Questions

Part I: The Covenant-Kingdom Connection

1. (a) What did God tell the Israelites they would be to Him if they obeyed His voice and kept His covenant? (Exodus 19:5b–6a)

    _____

    _____

(b) In the New Testament, what similar statement is made in reference to the church, due to Jesus' sacrifice on the cross and the blood of the new covenant? Complete the following:

Revelation 1:5b–6a: *"To Him who loved us and washed us from our sins in His*

own blood, and _____ _____ _____ _____

_____ _____ _____ _____ _____ _____

_____*…."*

2. If we live in obedience to God and under the shelter of the new covenant in Christ, what will be our spiritual position? (Deuteronomy 28:13a)

_____

Part II: The Priestly Ministry of Christ

We cannot effectively rule as kings until we have first learned to serve as priests. To do this, we must understand that our priestly ministry mirrors Christ's.

3. What did the writer of Hebrews call Jesus Christ? Complete the following:

Hebrews 3:1: *"…consider the* _____ *and* _____

_____ *of our confession, Christ Jesus."*

4. In the Old Testament, the priests functioned according to the order of Aaron, the first high priest under the law, and his descendants and successors. Yet the new covenant in Christ necessitated a new order of priesthood. According to what order is Jesus Christ's eternal priesthood? (Hebrews 5:6b)

_____

KEY DEFINITION: *Melchizedek* comes from the Hebrew name *Malkiy-Tsedeq*, which means "king of right" (STRONG, G3198, H4442), or king of "rightness," or "righteousness" (NASC, H6664). In the Old Testament, Melchizedek was the *"king of Salem"* and *"priest of God Most High"* to whom Abraham gave a tithe of everything he had. (See Genesis 14:18–19.)

REFLECTIONS ON THE PRIESTHOOD OF CHRIST

Melchizedek was a type, or foreshadower, of Jesus Christ, the righteous King who is also our High Priest. The two offices, which had operated together in Melchizedek, were separated in Israel under the law of Moses: the kingship was given to the tribe of Judah, and the priesthood was bestowed on the tribe of Levi.

In Jesus Christ, the kingship and priesthood were united once again. Jesus served as King and Priest on earth, and He was highly exalted by God the Father as King of Kings and Lord of Lords after His resurrection and ascension. On the basis of His priesthood, Jesus offered bread and wine during the Last Supper with His disciples as a symbol of His body and blood, which would be presented to God as a living sacrifice. (See, for example, Matthew 26:26–29.) He offered prayers, intercession, and His very self (see Hebrews 5:7; 9:14) to His heavenly Father by means of the Holy Spirit, constituting Himself both as the Priest who ministered the sacrifice and the Sacrifice itself. After making atonement for us, He entered the Holy of Holies in heaven on our behalf and as our predecessor (see Hebrews 6:19–20), so that we can now enter God's presence, also.

The Old Testament high priest was the mediator between God and man. Jesus has been mediating for the church as its High Priest for more than two thousand years—and He is our High Priest today. His work continues in force because no one can approach, communicate with, or bring offerings to God without the mediation of the High Priest. Therefore, we depend totally on Christ. (See Hebrews 7:24–25; 8:6.)

Part III: The Role of Priest in God's Kingdom in the Now

The roles of priest and king are always interconnected. Believers who rule and exercise dominion on earth have learned to serve as priests of almighty God. This sacred ministry operates in God's presence—the heavenly Holy of Holies—where His throne is located. We are members of God's spiritual priesthood, and our responsibilities center on offering up *"spiritual sacrifices"* (1 Peter 2:5) to Him. Let us look at some acts of spiritual sacrifice that we are to fulfill as priests in God's kingdom.

- **Present Our Bodies as Living Sacrifices**

5. (a) What kind of living sacrifices should we be? Complete the following:

Romans 12:1: "...*present your bodies a living sacrifice,* _____,

_____ _____ _____, *which is your reasonable service.*"

(b) Through whom must we offer up our sacrifices so that they may be acceptable to God? (1 Peter 2:5b)

_____

(c) What are we to do in conjunction with offering ourselves to God as living sacrifices? (Romans 12:2a)

_____

(d) When we do so, what will we *"prove"*? (Verse 12b)

_____

The New Testament concept of a priest is someone who presents spiritual sacrifices to God.

REFLECTIONS ON BEING A LIVING SACRIFICE

Since Jesus' sacrifice was complete when He offered His body on the cross, and since He already did the work of redemption, reconciliation, and restoration, the only thing left for us to do is to offer our bodies as a living sacrifice to God. The altar on which we sacrifice is not an object; rather, it is our heart—and the sacrifice is ourselves.

Presenting our bodies to God is a simple and practical act; there is nothing mystical about it. It means that from this day forward, we will no longer follow what the old nature or "self" wants, feels, or thinks. Rather, we will surrender our bodies to God's service. We will no longer offer our bodies to drugs, illicit sex, or selfish carnal pleasures, but we will live for eternal purposes as we do God's good and perfect will. This means that one of the benefits of presenting our bodies to the Lord and having our minds renewed is God carrying out His will in our lives.

+ **Offer Sacrifices of Praise and Worship**

6. (a) Why should we give praise to God? (Psalm 145:3a NIV)

_____

(b) Through Christ, how often are we to offer the sacrifice of praise to God? (Hebrews 13:15a)

_____

If we worship God only according to our feelings, we have not learned to praise Him.

+ **Do Good and Share with Others**

7. (a) What did Jesus say about how we are to treat other people? (Luke 6:35a)

_____

(b) What will happen if we give to others in various ways? (Verse 38a)

_____

_____

(c) Hebrews 13:16 refers to doing good and sharing as being *"sacrifices"* with which *"God is well pleased."* What will happen to the person who is generous toward others? What will happen to the person who *"refreshes"* others? (Proverbs 11:25 NIV)

_____

_____

God will empower us in the areas in which we surrender to Him.

+ **Present Physical Gifts and Offerings to God**

8. (a) The high priest under the law of Moses presented both sacrifices and gifts to God on behalf of the people, which the people themselves had provided out of their own resources. (See Hebrews 5:1.) What are some material sacrifices and gifts that we should present to God, which are His due? (Malachi 3:8b)

_____

(b) Once, when Jesus was in the temple, He noticed a poor widow putting two mites, or small coins, into the treasury. What statement did He make about her contribution, compared to the contributions of those who were rich? (Luke 21:3–4)

_____

_____

_____

(c) What guidelines for giving did the apostle Paul provide for us?
(2 Corinthians 9:7a)

_____

(d) What kind of *"giver"* does God love? (Verse 7b)

_____

Monetary offerings presented by believers are sacrifices of worship to God.

+ **Offer Prayer and Intercession**

9. (a) Christ's present ministry in heaven as High Priest includes making intercession on our behalf. (See Hebrews 7:25b.) Likewise, as we fulfill our ministry as priests unto God, what types of requests and remembrances are we to make on behalf of *"all men,"* including national leaders and all who are in authority? (1 Timothy 2:1)

_____

(b) In Matthew 6:9–13, Jesus taught His disciples to pray by giving them a prayer "template" that included essential elements of prayer. The words *"our"* and *"us"* in this prayer indicate that we are to pray these petitions in conjunction with other believers, and not just for our own lives. Record what we are to corporately ask for, following the example below:

Verse 9: <u>that people would "hallow," or reverence, God's name</u>

Verse 10: _____

Verse 11: _____

Verse 12: _____

Verse 13a: _____

10. What four designations did Peter use in referring to believers, reflecting our priestly ministry unto God? (1 Peter 2:9a)

_____

Intercessors rule on earth from the spirit realm.

Part IV: The Role of King in God's Kingdom in the Now

The "territory" of our allotted "kingdom," or sphere of influence, might be our family, our business, our community, our ministry, another realm of life, or a combination of some of the above. Yet, regardless of the size of our territories, we are kings over them, and we need to "extend our rods" and begin to rule, according to the guidance and power of the Holy Spirit.

+ **Rule with the Rod of Authority in Christ**

11. (a) What is announced in Psalm 110, indicating what God the Father will do on behalf of His Son Jesus? (Verse 2a)

_____

(b) Following this announcement, what decree did the Father give the Son? (Verse 2b)

_____

KEY DEFINITION: In biblical times, a rod was "a sign of authority, hence a scepter."[2] The rod is representative of a king's authority. After Jesus resurrected, ascended, and sat down on His throne in heaven, He gave us authority to use His "rod" over the nations and to extend His kingdom, carrying out the purpose and plans of the Father. (See, for example, Matthew 28:18–20.) We rule according to Jesus' rod of authority to expand the kingdom of God and to push back the kingdom of darkness in all its forms.

(c) Indicate the "rod of authority" that Jesus has given to believers to enable them to save, heal, and deliver others. Complete the following:

Mark 16:17–18: "[Jesus said,] *'And these signs will follow those who believe:* _____ _____ _____ *they will cast out demons; they will speak with new tongues;…they will lay hands on the sick, and they will recover.'*"

(d) Acts 3:1–9 recounts the healing of a lame man by Peter and John. What did Peter explain was the means through which the lame man was *"made strong,"* or healed? (Acts 3:16a)

_____

_____

The authority is in the name written on the rod, but it has no use until it is exercised.

+ **Rule Through Prayer**

Ruling through prayer is one way in which the roles of king and priest overlap. True power in the spirit realm is activated by those who know how to pray in order to establish the kingdom of God and cause His will to be done in their communities and nations.

12. (a) In the New Testament, we read how the prayers of believers ruled over a situation of persecution—even though they didn't know how effective their prayers would be! What did the believers do when the apostle Peter was imprisoned by King Herod, shortly after the king had killed James, the brother of John? (Acts 12:5b)

2. *The Zondervan Pictorial Bible Dictionary*, Merrill C. Tenney, gen. ed. (Grand Rapids, MI: Zondervan Publishing House, 1967), "Rod," 726.

(b) Whom did God send to supernaturally release Peter from prison, where he was bound with chains and guarded by four squads of soldiers? (Acts 12:7–11)

_____

(c) How did the believers respond when Peter suddenly showed up at the place where many of them had gathered together to pray for him? (Verse 16b)

_____

(d) Shortly thereafter, Herod sat on his throne and gave an oration to the people of Tyre and Sidon, who shouted, *"The voice of a god and not of a man!"* (See verses 21–22.) What happened to Herod, and why? (Verse 23)

_____

_____

(e) What occurred with the word of God following this incident? (Verse 24)

_____

Let us now explore three principles in relation to ruling through prayer.

Prayer Principle #1: Our Prayers Must Be Based on Scripture

13.   (a) God's will is written in His Word. What confidence can we have in God when we ask for something in prayer? (1 John 5:14b)

_____

(b) What do we have, if we know God hears our prayers? (Verse 15b)

_____

Prayer Principle #2: Our Prayers Must Correspond to a Rhema, or a Revealed Word from the Holy Spirit in the Here and Now

14. (a) As a proclamation of God's judgment of the Israelites' idolatry and other wickedness, what rhema did the prophet Elijah receive regarding rain in Israel, a rhema that he proclaimed to King Ahab? (1 Kings 17:1b)

    _____

    (b) A true rhema will not contradict God's written Word. Rather, the Bible will support it, and supernatural manifestations will confirm it. What warning in the law of Moses would Elijah likely have been familiar with as a confirmation of the rhema word he received? Complete the following:

    Deuteronomy 11:16–17: "*Take heed to yourselves, lest your heart be deceived, and you turn aside and serve other gods and worship them, lest the* LORD'*s anger be aroused against you, and He* _____ _____ _____ _____ _____

    _____ _____ _____ _____ _____, *and the land yield no produce, and you perish quickly from the good land which the* LORD *is giving you.*"

    (c) After three-and-a-half years without rain had passed, what new word did the Lord give Elijah? (1 Kings 18:1b)

    _____

    (d) What corresponding rhema did Elijah later communicate to Ahab? (Verse 41)

    _____

    (e) The above episode provides an example of how God's people have exercised His rule through obedience to His word, and prayer. The fulfillment of the above rhema took concentrated prayer on Elijah's part. (See verses 42–44.) What was the eventual result? (Verse 45)

    _____

(f) What encouragement did the apostle James give us that God can work through us to do His will, just as He worked through Elijah? Complete the following:

James 5:17a: "*Elijah was a man* _____ _____ _____ _____

_____."

(g) What kind of prayer avails much? (Verse 16b)

_____

Prayer Principle #3: Our Prayers Must Be Empowered by the Holy Spirit

15. (a) In Acts 4:23–30, Peter, John, and their companions prayed together, asking God to give them boldness to speak His word, and to heal and do signs and wonders in Jesus' name. What was the result? (Verse 31)

_____

_____

(b) In what other ways did the Holy Spirit answer their prayer? (Acts 5:12a, 14, 16b)

_____

_____

_____

16. How does the Holy Spirit help us in our weaknesses? (Romans 8:26b, 27b)

_____

_____

Conclusion

The world is waiting for us to go out and demonstrate that our supreme King and High Priest, Jesus Christ, lives today and that we are kings and priests in God's kingdom. People need us to show them practical solutions to their difficulties and to manifest the power and authority we have in Christ to rule over the works of the devil—to prove that the gospel of the kingdom is not mere theology, theory, or words, but that God's power can save people, heal their afflictions, and deliver them from bondage.

Dear friend, I challenge you to take your place in the kingdom as a priest of almighty God and as a king over the territory He has given you. From your position in Christ, seated with Him in the heavenly places, rule with authority, in the name of Jesus—whether in your home, business, ministry, church, neighborhood, city, or nation. From that place, bring God's kingdom of righteousness, peace, and joy to the earth, expanding His reign and manifesting miracles, signs, and wonders to destroy the works of the devil and to banish the kingdom of darkness!

Prayer of Activation

Holy Spirit, we ask You to enlighten the eyes of our understanding so that we may comprehend our calling as God's kings and priests under our Supreme King and High Priest, Jesus Christ. Heavenly Father, we present our bodies to You as a living sacrifice. We place ourselves in Your hands. Do with us as You wish, and send us wherever You want us to go. We will give You praise, tithes, and offerings. Empower us as we serve and intercede for other people, that they may come to know You and be freed from sin, guilt, and oppression. We take our rod of authority and begin to use it, right now. Anoint us as we expand Your kingdom on earth, today! Give us the grace to carry out our responsibilities as kings and priests before You, offering acceptable sacrifices and ruling according to Your will and Word. Amen!

Action Steps

+ Since we are the extension of the ministry of Jesus, who *"always lives to make intercession for* [us]" (Hebrews 7:25), we should make prayer and intercession on behalf of other people a priority. What an honor and privilege to be a priest of the living God! There are countless plans and purposes of God that cannot be carried out until we birth them through prayer. Let us align our prayers with Christ's prayers. Let us pray for the expansion of God's kingdom on earth and for the salvation of souls, as well as other spiritual needs. Ask the Holy Spirit to pray through you, according to God's will. (See Romans 8:26–27.)

+ As a kingdom ruler, start using your rod of authority through the name of Jesus. Demonstrate His reign with miracles, signs, wonders, and the casting out of demons.

Exercise rule in your own environment. Take authority over sickness in your body, lack in your finances, depression in your soul, and every attack of Satan. Remember that you are anointed and that God has given you the authority to do these things. Use the rod right now! It has the power to deliver you, your spouse, your natural and spiritual children, your ministry, your business, your community, and even your nation.

ENCOUNTERS WITH GOD'S KINGDOM

A Miraculous Healing of Thyroid Cancer and Nerve Damage

In Venezuela, a doctor named Betty Martínez was diagnosed with a cancerous tumor of the thyroid gland that was two-and-a-half centimeters (about one inch) long, and she underwent two surgeries. The first surgery showed that the cancer had metastasized to the lymph nodes in her neck. The second surgery, which should have taken only one-and-a-half hours, lasted eight hours due to complications. The surgeries did not produce the desired results, and, worst of all, certain nerves in Dr. Betty's spinal cord were affected. Consequently, she was unable to raise her left arm and was quickly losing all feeling on the left side of her face. She spent torturous sessions in therapy that left her feeling terrible and from which it took her a long time to recover. To make matters worse, three more tumors appeared. She needed more surgery and chemotherapy!

Dr. Betty said, "My God, I won't be able to endure this!" Her heart gave out, and she had a heart attack. After her recovery from the heart attack, and as she was preparing to have the next surgery, she was invited to a House of Peace (home fellowship ministry) affiliated with King Jesus Ministry, and she was told healing would be ministered to her. To this she said, "I have to see it to believe it." However, she was sick and tired of being ill and not finding a medical solution to her condition, so she accepted the invitation.

The entire group at the House of Peace joined in prayer for her, and the power of God enveloped her completely. She felt the three new tumors disappear instantly! Her joy was overflowing! Her life was radically transformed, so that she now testifies to her patients and prays for them in her office. She also preaches to her colleagues through her personal testimony. Many doctors are coming to the Lord through her witness and are imparting what they have received to their patients. Spectacular miracles are taking place. For example, cancer patients and people who are undergoing intensive therapy are being healed by the power of God.

Can we rule over our circumstances today? Of course! We are kings with God's authority and power to take dominion. Receive this word by faith! We must learn to rule over sickness and every evil thing through prayer.

Faith: The Currency of the Kingdom

"For we walk by faith, not by sight."
—2 Corinthians 5:7

Introduction

Faith is to the kingdom of God what currency is to a nation. In recent years, the strongest currencies in the world have been losing their value, purchasing power has fluctuated, and many people have felt financially insecure. Only the kingdom of God is unshakable. Its currency is always strong, and it allows us to acquire everything we need from the eternal realm.

Without faith it is impossible to please God (see Hebrews 11:6), and if we fail to please Him, we won't obtain anything from His kingdom. Of course, faith is not the only thing that pleases God—obedience, holiness, reverence, worship, fasting, and prayer also please Him, but none of these things has worth if it is practiced without faith. If we are to receive from what is in eternity, we must understand what faith is, how it functions, and how to walk according to it.

Study Questions

Part I: Where Faith Originates

1. How is faith described in the Scriptures? (Hebrews 11:1)

_____

KEY DEFINITION: The word *"faith"* in Hebrews 11:1 is translated from the Greek word *pistis*, among whose meanings are "credence," "moral conviction (of religious truth, or the truthfulness of God or a religious teacher), especially reliance upon Christ for salvation," "assurance," "belief," "faith," and "fidelity" (STRONG, G4102). *Pistis* comes from the root word *peitho*, which means "to persuade" and "to have confidence" (NASC, G3982). When we move in the spiritual realm, there is no natural, tangible evidence; we operate by internal spiritual discernment rather than physical proof or intellectual understanding.

2. How does faith come to us? (Romans 10:17)

God gave us faith as the avenue from the unseen world to the seen world.

---

3. God's Word feeds our spirits and fills our lives with an atmosphere of faith through which we may experience Christ's resurrection life and the power to build His kingdom. What truth did Jesus affirm in this regard? (Matthew 4:4)

4. What has God "*dealt*," or given, to each believer for his or her particular service to Him? (Romans 12:3b)

REFLECTIONS ON OUR MEASURE OF FAITH

This faith of which we are given a measure is a portion of God's own faith, which is supernatural. In Mark 11:22, Jesus told His disciples, "*Have faith in God.*" A more literal translation of this statement is "Have God's faith." Jesus was telling us that God grants us a portion of the faith that belongs to Him. Therefore, we all start our Christian lives with a measure of potent faith already given to us.

We must learn this indispensable spiritual truth: Faith originates in heaven, and it operates from there—above and beyond the natural world. This is why, to have faith, we must be born of God's Spirit, which gives us access to the heavenly realm. (See John 3:1–8.) It is impossible to be born again and not be activated in the supernatural.

---

5. When Jesus declared a person healed, or commanded a demon to leave someone, there was essentially no delay between the word of healing or deliverance and its

manifestation. On what basis did Jesus perform His miracles, which should be a model for our faith? Complete the following:

John 5:19: *"Jesus...said to them,...'The Son can do nothing of Himself, but _____ _____ _____ _____ _____ _____; for whatever*

He does, _____ _____ _____ _____ _____ _____

_____.'"

6. (a) Through our words, we "spend" our faith, or "put it into circulation," on earth. Every time we speak, we activate a spiritual exchange. What did the writer of Proverbs say are in the *"power of the tongue"*? (Proverbs 18:21a)

   _____

   (b) What kinds of words should we be "putting into circulation," and why? (Ephesians 4:29b)

   _____

   (c) List some types of "words"—whether prompted or given directly by the Holy Spirit—through which believers can edify one another. (1 Corinthians 14:26)

   _____

7. What biblical truth must we embrace so that we may "spend" the currency of faith in an effective manner? (Luke 1:37)

   _____

Faith is anchored in the invisible realm, which is superior to all that is visible. When we declare something by faith, from eternity, we bring it into existence.

REFLECTIONS ON CONFESSING GOD'S WORD

We make transactions using the spiritual currency of God's kingdom by declaring His Word in faith. We must make this a practice in our lives. However, let me caution you not to confuse faith with the act of confessing God's promises. In today's church, faith is often turned into a formula, so that some Christians tend to believe they will find a solution to their problems by simply repeating Bible verses. Faith is thereby reduced to "positive confession" rather than something activated by the *"living and powerful"* Word of God. (See Hebrews 4:12.) Remember that confessing what God has said feeds our faith, but it is not faith itself.

We cannot think like God unless we possess internal "knowing." Faith "sees" the invisible, believes the incredible, and receives the impossible.

Part II: How to Live and Move in "Now" Faith

God wants to move us into the dimension of faith that is in the here and now—for miracles, signs, wonders, and acceleration in the advancement of His kingdom. Let us examine the steps to living and moving in "now" faith.

+ **Operate Your Faith from a Place of Righteousness**

8. (a) Who will live by his faith? (Romans 1:17b; Habakkuk 2:4b)

    _____

    (b) In the gospel, how is the righteousness of God revealed? Complete the following:

    Romans 1:17a: "…*the righteousness of God is revealed* _____

    _____ _____ _____."

The law of righteousness makes faith operative; unrighteousness makes it inoperative.

+ **Walk by Faith, Not By Sight**

9. (a) God determines the purpose of something before He creates it, and He finishes everything in eternity before He starts it on earth. What does God declare in accordance with this reality? Complete the following:

Isaiah 46:10a: *"Declaring* _____ _____ _____ _____

_____ *, and* _____ _____

_____ _____ _____ _____ _____

_____ _____ *...."*

(b) How do we inherit the promises of God? (Hebrews 6:12b)

_____

REFLECTIONS ON WALKING BY FAITH

Second Corinthians 5:7 says, *"We walk by faith, not by sight."* The word *"sight"* represents the limitations of our natural environment, surroundings, circumstances, difficulties, obstacles, sicknesses, lack, impossibilities, and more. Such things are the opposite of faith. In order to rise above them, we must "see" a different reality and acquire a new perspective. If our thoughts are consumed by a hard situation, problem, or obstacle, we are not living by faith. The natural world is unstable, insecure, and temporal, but God does not change. When we walk by faith and not sight, our reality no longer depends on our environment or circumstances but on His eternal reality, and we become everything He has called us to be.

Faith is a continuous, supernatural walk with God in the now.

+ **Rise Above Human Reason Through the Spirit and the Word**

10. What are some ways in which the Holy Spirit enables us to rise above human reason so that we may live in the realm of faith? Complete the following:

John 16:13: *"When He, the Spirit of truth, has come,* _____ _____

_____ _____ _____ _____ _____ *; for He*

will not speak on His own authority, but whatever He hears He will speak; and _____

_____ _____ _____ _____ _____ *."*

11. (a) What does the *"entrance"* of God's words give? (Psalm 119:130)

_____

(b) What are some things for which the *"God-breathed"* Scriptures are useful? (2 Timothy 3:16b NIV)

_____

Faith is the ability to believe what reason finds nonsensical.

• Renounce the Spirit of Religion

12. (a) Religion enslaves people by raising mental strongholds that prevent God's fresh revelation from entering their hearts and minds. As a result, they often become legalists. What can our spiritual weapons, including the armor of God, mightily do? (2 Corinthians 10:4b)

_____

(b) We can rise above the spirit of religion in the same way that we rise above human reason and logic, paving the way for increased faith. To review, how do we do this? (Verse 5)

_____

_____

Everything to which we conform will become our reality and mind-set.

• Continually Walk in the Revealed Knowledge of God

13. (a) We must regularly read and/or listen to recordings of the Scriptures in order to feed our spirits and our faith, enabling us to receive and walk in God's revealed knowledge. In accordance with this necessity, what did the psalmist tell God he would do—practices that we, too, should engage in? (Psalm 119:15–16)

_____

_____

(b) Like the psalmist, what should we pray as we read God's Word? (Psalm 119:18)

_____

(c) We must not only learn and understand God's Word and receive revelation from the Holy Spirit, but we must also apply, in faith, what we have learned, understood, and received. What did the psalmist pray in agreement with this? (Psalm 119:33–34)

_____

_____

_____

Faith is based on knowledge.
The only parts of the Bible that will work for us are the ones we know.

+ **Stand Firm on God's Truth, Not on Facts**

14. What did Jesus say will happen if we abide in His Word, and thereby know the truth? (John 8:32)

_____

15. Record some truths of Scripture on which we can stand—if we are living in obedience to God's Word—rather than on the "facts" of various situations:

   (a) The fact is sickness. What is the truth of Scripture? (Isaiah 53:5b)

_____

   (b) The fact is a lack of finances. What is the truth of Scripture? (Philippians 4:19)

_____

   (c) The fact is depression. What is the truth of Scripture? (Isaiah 61:3a)

_____

_____

(d) The fact is that our difficulties are wearing us down. What is the truth of Scripture? (2 Corinthians 4:16–18a)

_____

_____

_____

_____

_____

Truth is the only thing that can defy facts because it is the highest level of reality and operates beyond facts. Facts are temporal, but faith is eternal.

✦ Maintain the Rhythm of Your Faith

As we have seen, each time we receive fresh revelation, we must put it into practice and experience it. This will enable us to continually maintain the "rhythm" of our faith. Otherwise, our faith will come to a standstill, and God's Word will be nullified in our lives, because it will exist beyond our level of obedience. An important way we can grow spiritually and maintain the rhythm of our faith is by diligently adding to our spiritual attributes through the power of the Holy Spirit.

16. (a) List the spiritual attributes that we should progressively acquire, beginning with our faith. (2 Peter 1:5b–7)

_____

(b) What will be the result if we abound in these attributes? (Verse 8)

_____

✦ Exercise Your Faith Through Love

17. (a) What truly *"avails"* in our relationship with God? (Galatians 5:6b)

_____

<u>KEY DEFINITION</u>: The Greek word translated *"working"* in Galatians 5:6 is *energeo*, which means "to be active, efficient" (STRONG, G1754), or "to be at work, to work, to do" (NASC, G1754). While righteousness makes faith operative, love energizes and activates it. Faith works through love because it functions according to the character of God. Faith that doesn't originate in love is like a clanging cymbal—pure noise without substance. (See 1 Corinthians 13:1.)

(b) What was poured out in our hearts when God gave us the Holy Spirit, enabling us to live according to the spiritual reality of Galatians 5:6? Complete the following:

Romans 5:5b: *"Now hope does not disappoint, because _____ _____*

_____ _____ has been poured out in our hearts by the Holy Spirit who was given

to us."

Every miracle and healing that Jesus performed was motivated by compassion.

Conclusion

If we conform to what the natural world says, we will accept it as being the last word, and it will rule over us. When such thinking becomes established in our hearts, we are not able to receive the supernatural, and we become magnets for sickness, poverty, lack, depression, and pain. We must establish in our hearts the truths that go beyond all temporal reality so that we may receive in the now everything that Jesus provided for us on the cross!

God designed you to be saved, righteous, holy, at peace, joyful, blessed, healthy, free, prosperous, and more. You don't have to wait for someday in the future to be saved, healed, and prosperous. Faith is "now" to provide practical solutions to the problems we face every day. But we also have to intentionally exercise our faith daily. Religion might have deactivated you from genuine faith, but today, as an apostle of God, I reactivate you in God's faith to receive revelation and miracles right now. Reject empty tradition and religion as you continue to be transformed by the renewing of your mind and as you seize true faith!

Prayer of Activation

Perhaps you have been exercising your faith and have witnessed the power of God to some extent, but you want to enter the dimension of faith in the here and now in order to revolutionize your environment. I invite you to pray the following prayer out loud:

Heavenly Father, we confess that Jesus Christ is our Lord and Savior. We believe that He is seated at Your right hand, that we are seated with Him in the heavenly places, and that we have received a measure of Your faith. From this day forward, we will live and walk in the divine supernatural. We have legal access to the invisible realm, and the supernatural is normal to us because we have Your perspective, in which anything is possible. Signs, miracles, and wonders are our lifestyle. By faith, we bring Your kingdom to earth. We call the eternal realm to the physical realm! We heal the sick, cast out demons, release prophetic words, deliver the captives, and preach the gospel of the kingdom with power. Father, we know that You give us the grace to do all these things, in Jesus' name. Amen!

Action Steps

+ Establish a daily practice of reading the Bible and/or listening to recorded Scriptures.

+ Commit to using, exercising, and investing your faith. Start by believing for small things. Give your faith a specific assignment. For example, believe for a small amount of money, healing for a headache, or something else you need. If your faith is mature, go beyond these small requests and pray for the salvation of souls, transformed hearts, creative miracles, deliverance, profitable business contracts, the multiplication of the gifts of the Holy Spirit, supernatural favor with people in authority, and more. The most important thing is to live by your faith and to exercise it continuously so that you will maintain its rhythm and keep moving to greater levels of faith.

+ Decide right now to rise above the places, people, and things that keep you from walking and growing in faith. Begin to edify a new atmosphere of faith in your life and home. Do not conform to the temporal; seek God and enter the spirit realm, where faith can change your reality. Sickness, problems, adversity, and trials were never ordained to be permanent. Yet we have learned to tolerate them, and we have turned them into something permanent by saying, "*My* sickness; *my* pain; *my* lack; *my* depression...." We speak as if these things belonged to us, when they don't. Take authority over them in faith, right now, in the name of Jesus!

ENCOUNTERS WITH GOD'S KINGDOM

Healed of HIV

Vene Labans of South Africa was diagnosed with HIV six years before King Jesus Ministry held a conference on the supernatural in East London, South Africa. A couple of days prior to the meetings, a friend of Vene's invited her to attend. She was reluctant but decided to go. On Sunday, Apostle Maldonado preached on "The Gospel of the Now," saying that, if we believe, we will receive our miracle. Then he made an altar call for those who were HIV-positive or had cancer. Vene approached the altar, willing to use her faith to be healed. A member of Apostle Maldonado's ministry team declared healing over her, and she felt heat flowing through her body. The following day, she was scheduled to go to the clinic to obtain her monthly medication, but a friend insisted she should be tested, instead, to confirm her healing. So, Vene asked for a new test. To the glory of God, the results were negative!

In one day, Vene's life was completely transformed. Her sickness was temporary; it came to its end when she encountered the power of God. "This conference has completely changed my life; it has given me joy, health, and everything I needed!" she said.

Study 11

Demonstrations of Kingdom Power Here and Now

"And my speech and my preaching were not with persuasive words of human wisdom, but in demonstration of the Spirit and of power."
—1 Corinthians 2:4

Introduction

Jesus taught His disciples to pray, *"For Yours is the kingdom and the power and the glory forever. Amen"* (Matthew 6:13). Although each facet of God's dominion is distinct, it always works in conjunction with the others: the kingdom is the rule of heaven, the power is the ability of heaven, and the glory is the atmosphere of heaven. God is calling us to exercise His kingdom rule, demonstrate His power, and manifest His glorious presence on earth—here and now!

While it is important for us to teach people about the kingdom, it is even more powerful to demonstrate it. If we fail to act on what we teach, then we are not being true to ourselves or to others. Jesus Christ demonstrated the kingdom by both teaching and acting with power. And He gave us the ability to do the same through the Holy Spirit.

Study Questions

Part I: Knowledge Should Lead to Supernatural Experience

1. It is not enough just to hear the *"word"* of the kingdom. That word must be planted in our hearts so it can bear fruit. Indicate what keeps some people from establishing God's Word in their lives, by completing the following:

    Matthew 13:19: *"When anyone hears the word of the kingdom, and _____ _____ _____ _____, then the wicked one comes and snatches away what was sown in his heart."*

KEY DEFINITION: The word *"understand"* in Matthew 13:19 is translated from the Greek word *suniemito*. It literally means "to put together" and indicates mental comprehension that leads to godly living. (See STRONG, G4920.) In other words, it is an understanding of the knowledge of God that leads to a transformed life.

2. (a) What should we humbly accept? (James 1:21b NIV)

_____

_____

(b) Doing what God's Word says, rather than just reading it or listening to it, will help us to understand His Word and establish it within us, so that we are transformed. (See James 1:22.) To whom did the apostle James compare the person who just listens to the Word without applying it to his life? (Verses 23b–24 NIV)

_____

_____

REFLECTIONS ON EXPERIENCING THE SUPERNATURAL

The *"word of the kingdom"* (Matthew 13:19) is like seed. When we receive a revelation from God, allowing it to be implanted within us, it imparts the power that enables us to obey it. But when we do not understand or accept a word from God, it cannot be implanted within us. Instead, it is like seed that gets scattered on the side of the road; it lands on shallow soil and is vulnerable to being eaten by birds and other animals passing by. In a spiritual sense, this is what happens when the enemy comes and steals the word away from us.

Since the human mind is very limited and cannot embrace the greatness of God, we must allow Him to demonstrate in visible form what we believe and proclaim. Each time God gives us knowledge or revelation, He wants us to have personal contact with His kingdom and power. Therefore, anytime we receive a word that inspires us, challenges us, and encourages us to seek more of Him, we are not to remain where we are but are to take the next step and experience the reality of that word, which always leads us to Him.

When we enter into an experience with God based on what we learn from His Word or from a rhema we have received, our perspective changes. We gain greater spiritual depth, and we are able to explain God's Word with better clarity and insight. We no longer describe God and His truths as external observers. It's almost as if we are within the truth itself, or a part of it.

We must know God to demonstrate His works.

Part II: The Balance Between the Spirit and the Word

Jesus was able to teach and demonstrate the message of God's kingdom because He was continually in contact with the Father. His words and actions had the life of God in them. The pattern in Scripture is that God sends His Spirit before sending His word, because His word has power on earth only if it originates from the atmosphere of His presence. A word of God operates on earth when He speaks (either a word from the written Scriptures or a rhema), and the power of God operates when He acts. But a word from God will not demonstrate the kingdom on earth until we receive a revelation of it. God's Spirit and His word always work together.

3. (a) As an example of the pattern in Scripture discussed above, what occurred before God began to create life on the earth? (Genesis 1:2b)

    _____

    (b) Following this, what words did God speak, and what transpired? (Verse 3)

    _____

4. What two things did Jesus say are essential for a person to know in order to have accurate spiritual understanding? (Mark 12:24b)

    _____

People will spiritually dry up and die unless the Holy Spirit moves in them.

---

5. Manifestations from the Holy Spirit are revelations that are discerned by our natural senses, enabling us to see and/or hear tangible evidence of God's kingdom, power, and glory. On the day of Pentecost, how did the Holy Spirit tangibly demonstrate God's kingdom to Jesus' followers and to the multitude in Jerusalem through manifestations of both sight and sound, Spirit and word? (Acts 2:2–4)

_____

_____

_____

Part III: Purposes of Demonstrating God's Kingdom Here and Now

Let us now turn to the purposes of demonstrating God's kingdom, to make sure we understand the main reasons why He desires to manifest His eternal realm on earth and why it is essential for us to seek first His kingdom. (See Matthew 6:33.)

+   **Purpose #1: So Our Faith Will Be Founded on the Power of God**

6. How did Paul say he presented his speech and preaching to the Corinthians as he announced the gospel to them, so that their faith would not be in the wisdom of men but in the power of God? Complete the following:

1 Corinthians 2:4: "*And my speech and my preaching were not with persuasive words*

of human wisdom, but _____ _____ _____

_____ _____ _____ _____ _____·...."

We can demonstrate God only when we have experienced Him.

+   **Purpose #2: To Establish a Kingdom Context for God's Power**

7. (a) The power of God always comes with the purpose of building and expanding His kingdom. Recall what Jesus spoke of to His followers, after His resurrection but before His ascension, to prepare them for the coming of the Holy Spirit at Pentecost. (Acts 1:3b)

_____

(b) What did Jesus tell His followers that they should *"tarry,"* or wait, to receive? (Luke 24:49)

_____

(c) Recall what kingdom purpose resulted from their receiving this thing, as Peter boldly proclaimed the gospel. (Acts 2:41)

_____

(d) Recall what miracle occurred shortly thereafter as a further demonstration that the kingdom of God was present among them. (Acts 3:1–8)

_____

Receiving "Pentecost" without kingdom power is merely one more Christian experience.

+ **Purpose #3: To Restore People and Things to God's Original Design, thus Reestablishing Spiritual Order**

8. (a) What was wrong with the woman whom Jesus saw in the synagogue, and with what symptoms did her problem manifest? (Luke 13:11)

_____

(b) How long had the woman suffered from this problem? (Verse 11)

_____

(c) Who had *"bound"* this woman for so long—an example of his usurping the "territory" of a person's life in order to establish his kingdom of darkness there? (Verse 16)

_____

(d) When Jesus healed this woman, what did He say was His reason for doing so, indicating that He was restoring God's kingdom to a woman of faith? Complete the following:

Luke 13:16: *"So ought not this woman, _____ _____*

_____ _____ _____, whom Satan has bound;

think of it; for eighteen years, be loosed from this bond on the Sabbath?"

+ **Purpose #4: To Establish Kingdom Structure**

The structure with which the Holy Spirit establishes and builds the kingdom is the structure of relationships. It is not rules, traditions, or statutes—founded on human ideas and purposes—established by denominations or churches whose supreme goal is to elevate order. If a structure is rigid, it will lead to extremes that prevent the Holy Spirit from moving. At that point, God will withdraw His presence, and the only thing left will be formality. Every kingdom manifestation must be demonstrated within a structure of relational order and purpose.

9. (a) What did Jesus pray that describes His relationship and oneness with the Father? Complete the following:

John 17:21: *"...that they all may be one, as _____, _____,*

_____ _____ _____, _____ _____ _____ _____."

(b) What did Jesus tell His disciples would result if they remained in unbroken relationship with Him by abiding in Him and having His words abide in them? (John 15:7b)

_____

_____

(c) Before He returned to heaven, Jesus told His disciples that He would send them a *"Helper"* (John 15:26; 16:7)—the Holy Spirit. While the Spirit used to be *"with"* them, where would He dwell after He was sent to them? (John 14:17b)

_____

10. (a) What did Jesus pray to the Father for all believers? Complete the following:

John 17:23: *"I in them, and You in Me;* _____ _____ _____

_____ _____ _____ _____ _____ *, and*

_____ _____ _____ _____ _____

_____ _____ _____ _____ _____ *, and have loved*

them as You have loved Me."

(b) How did Paul describe the oneness that believers share in Christ through the Holy Spirit? (1 Corinthians 12:13)

_____

_____

_____

(c) What did Paul say about believers' diverse gifts and different ministries? (Verses 4–5)

_____

_____

(d) Having harmonious, mutually beneficial relationships in the church is essential because we believers will inevitably influence one another, and we need the kingdom structure of relationships to enable us to achieve spiritual growth. As one illustration of these realities, how should older women in the church act, and what should they do, according to the apostle Paul? (Titus 2:3–4)

_____

_____

> ### *When Jesus ministered on earth, He taught and established a flexible structure for the kingdom based on relationships.*

+ **Purpose #5: To Confront and Bind Satan and His Demons**

11. (a) What authority did Jesus give to His disciples? Complete the following:

Luke 10:19: *"Behold, I give you the authority to trample on serpents and scorpions,*

and _____ _____ _____ _____ _____ _____

_____, *and nothing shall by any means hurt you."*

(b) What did Jesus say about the *"gates of Hades,"* or the forces of darkness, in relation to the church? (Matthew 16:18b)

_____

+ **Purpose #6: To Bring Judgment and Mercy**

12. (a) Demonstrations of God's kingdom can bring either judgment or mercy, as people variously reject them or accept them. For example, when Moses delivered the Israelites from slavery, the manifestations of God's power brought judgment on Egypt and mercy to Israel—destruction for one and freedom for the other. Similarly, what is the fragrance of Christ like for those who are perishing? (2 Corinthians 2:15–16a)

_____

(b) What is the fragrance of Christ like for those who are being saved? (Verse 16b)

_____

(c) What did the author of Lamentations say to illustrate how often God extends His *"mercies"* and *"compassions"* (Lamentations 3:22) to His people? (Verse 23a)

_____

+ ### Purpose #7: To Confirm That We Are Legitimate Witnesses of Christ

13. Recall the statement that Jesus made about the works that those who believed in Him would do. (John 14:12)

_____

_____

+ ### Purpose #8: To Establish Kingdom Expansion by Spiritual Force

14. God's kingdom cannot be established without forceful demonstrations of His power. As we have seen, such power is necessary to uproot and cast out the kingdom of darkness from a person or a place. What statement did Jesus make about the kingdom of heaven in this regard? (Matthew 11:12b)

_____

Conclusion

We must present the gospel with supernatural proofs demonstrating that Jesus lives and that His resurrection power is for today! Most people are not interested in us, our great knowledge, or the nice words we speak. They are interested in the bottom line: Do our words lead to supernatural works? Does our knowledge lead to an experience with God? Does our revelation produce a manifestation of His power? Does our theology bring healing to the sick, deliverance to the oppressed, prosperity to the poor, and repentance to the sinner? Does our testimony transform lives? We must live—and, just as important, we must disciple other Christians—on the basis of the revelation of God's Word combined with demonstrations that support its teaching.

Jesus' disciples were common people who did extraordinary deeds by the power of God. The coming of the Holy Spirit was not just a historic event in the first century. It can take place in the here and now, if we have the faith to receive it. God is looking for common people who believe in His Word and act upon it—whose minds are open to the reality of His power and glory and can bring these facets of His dominion from the invisible realm to the here and now!

Prayer of Activation

Dear Jesus, we are willing and available to go and demonstrate Your kingdom here and now. We ask You to give us Your supernatural grace to take risks and be bold in order to manifest Your power and glory. We ask Your Holy Spirit to come upon us and empower us now to do the works of the kingdom. Lord Jesus, by faith, wherever we go—to our schools, to our jobs, to restaurants, to sporting events, to malls, on vacation trips, or anywhere else—we will pray for the sick, the oppressed, and the captives, and we will deliver them in Your name. Those who haven't received salvation or the baptism in the Holy Spirit will receive it by Your power! We submit our wills and our hearts to You right now. In Your name, amen.

Action Steps

+ A believer who has a kingdom mentality is one who obeys the voice of God, putting into practice the spiritual truths he learns. What truths about the kingdom have you learned but not put into practice? Write down two or three kingdom truths that you haven't yet acted on and begin to obey them by faith right now. Keep a record of what happens as you follow through in obedience.

+ The more we respond in faith to the revelation God gives us, thereby experiencing His presence and power, the more we will grow in our ability to testify with manifestations of the kingdom to support our words, so that we can be credible witnesses of Jesus Christ. When we release the same power through which we have been saved, delivered, and healed, we can create a spiritual revolution, bringing salvation, deliverance, and healing to others. To do this, start at the beginning, with your salvation. Tell people what happened to you the day you were born again. Next, tell them how you have changed since that day. No one else can communicate your testimony like you. Only you can speak with absolute certainty about how you have been transformed. As you testify, the power of God will manifest, because you will be a legitimate witness. Share your testimony today. Then, as you receive other demonstrations of God's power in your life, share those with others, as well, so that people can be transformed, healed, and delivered!

ENCOUNTERS WITH GOD'S KINGDOM

Unborn Baby Receives Creative Miracle of New Kidney

At a miracle crusade held at King Jesus Ministry, Apostle Maldonado preached about the power of God and then ministered that power to others in a demonstrable way. Among those attending the meeting was a woman named Madeline who was pregnant and had received a bad diagnosis concerning her baby. At her first sonogram, the medical personnel had detected that her baby was missing its right kidney. Madeline was sad but began to pray for a miracle. The following month, she had another sonogram, and the doctors confirmed that the baby's right kidney had not formed. But Madeline did not give up. She continued to fight the good fight of faith. (See 1 Timothy 6:12.)

In the midst of this distressing situation, she attended the healing crusade, believing for a miracle. Apostle Maldonado gave an altar call for everyone who needed a creative miracle, and Madeline was one of the first to respond. He declared the word, and she took hold of it, crying and believing that God had done the miracle. During the ninth month of her pregnancy, when she went to have her last sonogram, the doctor told her he did not understand what had happened. What had not existed before was there now: the baby's right kidney had appeared! To the glory of God, after the birth, Madeline joyfully and gratefully testified that her daughter was healthy and had all of her organs. The supernatural power of the kingdom had performed a creative miracle that medical science was unable to produce.

Study 12

KINGDOM EXPANSION BY SPIRITUAL FORCE

"Be strong in the Lord and in the power of His might."
—Ephesians 6:10

Introduction

The early church proclaimed the gospel with remarkable results. However, most of the believers stayed within a limited sphere for the first few years. Many of them were situated in Jerusalem. I believe the early Christians remained where they were for a period of time because, at first, they lacked the revelation to go to the whole world with the gospel—the revelation that the Great Commission is global. (See, for example, Matthew 28:18–20.) It was to start in Jerusalem, but then it was to extend to *all Judea and Samaria, and to the end of the earth"* (Acts 1:8).

A similar lack of revelation is hindering the church from fulfilling its mandate today. Many believers are merely remaining where they are. Apparently, they do not feel spiritually ready or "mature" enough to go out to their communities and beyond, proclaiming the gospel of the kingdom with visible manifestations. In the meantime, the world remains lost, and people are dying and going to hell. If we wait until we are "mature" enough before we demonstrate the kingdom, we will never be ready, because there will always be one more thing in our lives that needs to change. Yet, if we are in the place spiritually where we can receive God's revelation, power, and glory and demonstrate them with visible manifestations, our lives will surely change. For the most part, character and the exercise of spiritual power grow together. What we really need is a revelation of Jesus' commandment of global kingdom expansion. God baptizes us in His Spirit for the purpose of receiving His power—and we receive His power to enable us to go and demonstrate His kingdom to the world in the now!

Study Questions

Part I: We Must Have a Revelation to Go into All the World

1. What global vision and command did Jesus give His disciples? (Mark 16:15)

   _____

2. As we learned in the introduction to this study, many of the early Christians remained in Jerusalem for some years after Christ ascended to heaven. What caused most of these believers to move beyond Jerusalem into Judea and Samaria with the gospel message, in fulfillment of Jesus' command? Complete the following:

   Acts 8:1, 4: *"At that time* ____ _____ _____ *arose against the church which was at Jerusalem; and they were all scattered throughout the regions of Judea and Samaria, except the apostles.…Therefore those who were scattered*

   _____ _____ _____

   _____ _____.*"*

3. (a) In one of His parables, to what did Jesus compare the kingdom of heaven? (Matthew 25:14b)

   _____

   _____

   (b) What did the man in the parable entrust to each of his servants, and by what criteria did he do so? (Verse 15a)

   _____

   (c) What did this man do immediately after entrusting these things to his servants, thus leaving the servants to use their own initiative with what they had been given? (Verse 15b)

   _____

Every kingdom principle is rooted in the law of increase and multiplication.

(d) When the man returned, what did he say to the servants who had gained additional talents by investing what they had been given? (Matthew 25:21, 23)

_____

_____

_____

(e) What did the man say should be done with the talent of the servant who had been wicked and lazy and had not gained any return or interest on what he had been given? (Verse 28)

_____

(f) How did Jesus sum up His parable of the talents? Complete the following:

Verse 29: "For to everyone who has, _____ _____ _____

_____, and _____ _____ _____

_____; but from him who does not have, _____

_____ _____ _____ _____ _____ _____

_____."

We must multiply what God gives us. Otherwise, we will lose it.

REFLECTIONS ON KINGDOM EXPANSION

In the Old Testament, God did not give the Promised Land to the Israelites all at once, because the people could not occupy all the territory immediately. He gave them whatever territory the soles of their feet touched. (See Deuteronomy 11:24; Joshua 1:3.) This is how He positioned them for kingdom expansion. He will do the same for us.

God gives each of us kingdom "territory," grace, anointing, favor, a measure of faith, authority, power, gifts, talents, finances, influence, and more that we are called to exercise and expand. Depending on our faithfulness, and our stewardship of what He has given us, He will increase our blessings or take them away. If we are continually on the offensive in terms of spiritual growth and movement, God will give us the increase and supply all our needs. His responsibility as a Father is to give us what we need. When He gives us more than that, it is for the purpose of blessing others with it. Those who operate according to a kingdom mentality invest and multiply everything God gives them.

Increase comes while we are in the process of expanding the kingdom.

Part II: The Enemy's Plan to Contain the Kingdom

Even as we endeavor to be faithful to God and to extend His rule on earth, the enemy tries to contain the expansion of the kingdom, and he uses human beings in his schemes to derail God's purposes.

4. (a) When Jesus spoke to His disciples about His forthcoming death and resurrection, what did Satan apparently prompt Peter to say in rebuke to Jesus? (Matthew 16:22b)

    _____

    (b) Recall what Jesus said when resisting Satan's temptation to avoid the cross. (Verse 23b)

    _____

    _____

5. (a) At a later time, Jesus told Peter that Satan had *"asked"* for him so that he could *"sift* [him] *as wheat"* (Luke 22:31). This was apparently the enemy's attempt to contain and perhaps destroy the future leader of the church. What did Jesus assure Peter that He had done for him, and why? (Verse 32a)

    _____

(b) What did Jesus tell Peter that he should do once he had returned to Jesus?
(Luke 22:32b)

_____

REFLECTIONS ON SATAN'S PLAN OF CONTAINMENT

Satan is always implementing his plan of containment to stop the advancement of God's kingdom. This means that we are in a continuous war against a spirit of suppression. We should not be surprised when every forward movement we make for the kingdom is countered by difficulties, obstacles, and persecution. The enemy will try to bind us and hold us back. He will confine us to one place, situation, or circumstance—in our personal lives, our ministry, our business, or any other arena where we are actively involved in extending the kingdom. Primarily, the enemy tries to confine us by tempting us to succumb to complacency and passivity. *Complacency* refers to self-gratification—pleasing the desires of the flesh or seeking personal gain with egocentrism and selfishness. *Passivity* refers to the state of being totally indifferent when evil takes over. It is an attitude of tolerance in which we allow the enemy to gain ground for his kingdom of darkness, never doing anything about it. (See, for example, Revelation 3:16.) The only solutions to such attitudes and behavior are spiritual breakthroughs in the power of the Holy Spirit. A breakthrough is a sudden intervention of God that takes us through—and beyond—whatever is preventing us from crossing over into new territory for God's kingdom and pushing out the kingdom of darkness. God will empower us to defeat the enemy and to remove and destroy the walls of sickness, poverty, and oppression that try to contain us!

Part III: Steps to Receiving a Spiritual Breakthrough

6. Just before Paul listed the elements of the *"armor of God,"* with which we can *"stand against the wiles of the devil"* (Ephesians 6:11), what did he urge believers to be? (Verse 10)

_____

The power of God in the area of spiritual warfare is called "might."

<u>KEY DEFINITION</u>: The word *"might"* in Ephesians 6:10 is translated from the Greek word *ischys*, meaning "forcefulness." In addition to "might," *ischys* indicates "ability," "power," and "strength" (STRONG, G2479). This concept of might can be compared to the military strength and resources of a great nation. A "spirit of might," or "breakthrough anointing," uses the strength of the kingdom of heaven and its almighty God, whose arsenal, strategies, and advance forces are deployed to destroy the enemy's plan of containment and to extend the territory of God's kingdom on earth. A breakthrough anointing enables us to increase, multiply, expand, or enlarge what God has given us.

REFLECTIONS ON SPIRITUAL BREAKTHROUGH

If we are to possess everything that Jesus won for us, we must fight the enemy in the power of God's might, expanding His kingdom by spiritual force. To receive a spiritual breakthrough, we have to be militant in exercising kingdom principles. This is a spiritual matter, and it applies to all of us—whether our natural personality is to be assertive or quiet. Passivity will leave us spiritually wounded instead of securing our breakthroughs. We must be ruthless with the enemy—he wants to destroy us! Demonic strongholds will tremble and fall away as we push against them in God's power. By the strength of the indwelling Holy Spirit and His supernatural weapons, we are enabled to break though the enemy's containment. In the process, we grow stronger to fulfill our role in the kingdom.

The purpose of a spiritual breakthrough is the expansion of the kingdom.

Let us now explore the steps to receiving a spiritual breakthrough.

+ **Refuse to Tolerate the Situation**

7. (a) Since our enemy *"walks about like a roaring lion, seeking whom he may devour,"* what preventive actions should we take against his schemes? (1 Peter 5:8a)

_____

(b) How should we respond to Satan when he attacks our health, our finances, our marriage, or anything else in our lives? (Verse 9a)

_____

(c) What did Peter pray that God would do for believers in such circumstances? Complete the following:

1 Peter 5:10: *"But may the God of all grace…after you have suffered a while,*

_____, _____, _____,

_____ _____ _____."

When a spiritual breakthrough takes place, our old mentality of limitation changes to a mentality of expansion.

+ **Be Filled with Righteous Indignation**

8. What spiritual instruction did Paul quote from Psalm 4:4, which we should follow when exercising righteous indignation against evil? (Ephesians 4:26a NIV)

   _____

9. When David was filled with righteous indignation against Goliath, what did he say about this enemy of Israel? (1 Samuel 17:26b)

   _____

10. (a) What was Paul's attitude toward the evil spirit who had possessed the Philippian slave girl, causing her to follow Paul around and make a commotion wherever he went? Complete the following:

   Acts 16:18a: *"And this she did for many days. _____ _____,*

   _____ _____…."

   (b) What action did Paul take in his righteous indignation against the evil spirit? (Verse 18b)

   _____

To establish your authority in any place, you must always declare the name of Jesus.

✦ Exercise "Spiritual Violence"

To be spiritually violent means to fight against the devil and his demons—not to become angry with God or other people, and not to become physically violent. Otherwise, our violence will neither be from God nor be holy. Spiritual violence is to be exerted against injustice, sickness, poverty, depression and all the other works of the devil.

11. (a) As we learned in the previous study, what statement did Jesus make about being "violent," or forceful, against the kingdom of darkness? (Matthew 11:12b)

_____

(b) When discussing how to defeat the enemy, Jesus compared Satan to a *"strong man."* What did He say we must do first in order to enter this "strong man's" house for the purpose of plundering his goods, or taking back the territory Satan has gained on earth? (Matthew 12:29a)

_____

✦ Offer Glorious, Spontaneous Praise to God

An important way of invading the kingdom of darkness is to sing songs under the inspiration of the Holy Spirit—and to continue to sing them until a spirit of might comes upon us and we experience a supernatural breakthrough.

12. (a) In Psalm 40, what did David say God had put in him? (Verse 3a NIV)

_____

(b) What did David say would happen when people saw (and heard) him expressing it? (Verse 3b NIV)

_____

(c) When the writer of Psalm 96 encouraged us to *"sing to the Lord a new song!"* (verse 1), what else did he encourage us to proclaim and declare? (Verses 2b–3)

_____

(d) In Psalm 98, what did the psalmist state as his reason for singing a new song to the Lord? (Verse 1)

_____

_____

(e) What three kinds of songs did the apostle Paul encourage believers to sing as a way of spiritually edifying one another? (Ephesians 5:19a; Colossians 3:16a)

_____

(f) What were believers to do in their hearts? (Ephesians 5:19b)

_____

When you have an experience with the power of God,
it will transform you within and without.

Part IV: Demonstrate the Kingdom of Power Here and Now

13. (a) For what reason did Jesus choose and appoint us for the kingdom? (John 15:16a)

_____

(b) What will God the Father do for us as we fulfill this appointed role? (Verse 16b)

_____

14. What promise and command did Jesus give us in order to establish and expand His kingdom government throughout the world? (Acts 1:8)

_____

_____

15. What message of kingdom expansion did God give His people through Isaiah? (Isaiah 54:2–3)

_____

_____

_____

_____

16. (a) What proclamation did Isaiah make about the increase of King Jesus' government and peace? (Isaiah 9:7a)

_____

(b) With what will Jesus' government be ordered and established forever? Complete the following:

Isaiah 9:7b: "…_to order it and establish it_ _____ _____

_____ _____ _from that time forward, even forever._"

17. (a) To sum up this Bible study course, what message are Jesus' followers to proclaim to the world? (Matthew 10:7b)

_____

(b) What evidences of the kingdom are we to manifest as we do this? (Verse 8a)

_____

Conclusion

Through this Bible study course, you have been equipped with the revelation of God's kingdom of power here and now. As you diligently seek God and yield your life to the Holy Spirit, you will receive God's empowerment and baptism of fire, igniting you to manifest His kingdom wherever you go—ruling over sickness, sin, demons, poverty, and death.

God created us to go into the world with all the gifts, abilities, and blessings He has bestowed on us so that we can extend and multiply His kingdom on earth. As we do, He will increase our faith, power, and blessings, enabling us to continue to enlarge His kingdom in the world. To extend God's domain, the church as a whole must function like a kingdom embassy to people in every town, city, and nation as we go to every tribe, race, and ethnic group in the world. We are to start new churches, ministries, businesses, and other ventures that demonstrate God's supernatural power and multiply the gifts He's given us, so that we can win souls, make disciples, heal the sick, deliver the oppressed, and help others who are in need. We cannot wait for the enemy to assault us before we take action against him. Instead, we are to be in permanent "attack mode," bringing forth great breakthroughs by God's spirit of might.

God's heart is for the whole world, for the globalization of His gospel. Are you willing to push forward in the power of the Spirit so that you may enter into greater dimensions of anointing, glory, power, authority, revelation, provision, and more? Are you willing to expand the influence of your family, ministry, business, or organization for the sake of the kingdom of God? Decide today—the challenge of bringing His kingdom to earth is here and now!

Prayers of Activation

If you have not yet received Jesus as your Lord and Savior, I want to give you another opportunity to do so right now. Pray the prayer found in the "Prayer of Activation" section at the end of study 1. You will not be able to receive breakthroughs and expand the kingdom if you are not yet a citizen of the kingdom. Don't wait any longer!

If you have just prayed to be born again and enter the kingdom of God, or if you have previously accepted Christ but have not yet received the baptism in the Holy Spirit, pray the following so that you may be filled with the Spirit, with the evidence of speaking in other tongues. Remember that the purpose of being baptized with the Spirit is to receive supernatural power to overcome sin, temptation, sickness, poverty, demons, and death, and to have victory in any other adverse circumstance of life.

Heavenly Father, we are Your children, and we ask You to fill us with Your precious Holy Spirit. As the Spirit gives us utterance, we now start speaking in other tongues.

Continue praying with the expectation that, right now, you will speak in a heavenly language.

If you have already received Jesus and been baptized in the Spirit but want God to use you in ever-increasing ways for His kingdom, pray the following:

Heavenly Father, we are Your beloved children. We are kings and priests under Your authority who rule over our territories in Your kingdom. We are warriors, having Your spirit of might to break down Satan's walls of containment and receive Your breakthroughs for the greater expansion of Your kingdom. Live in us today, and let Your Spirit move in our lives. Let our hearts always be receptive and obedient to Your purpose and will. May Your kingdom come and Your will be done on earth as it is in heaven—in the here and now, and for all eternity. Amen and amen!

Action Steps

+ Perhaps you feel like you are spinning your wheels or have come up against an immovable wall in your life, so that you don't seem to be making any progress. In such a situation, you should check your motivations and ask God to reveal any attitude or behavior that is blocking your relationship with Him and hindering your spiritual advancement. If He reveals anything, immediately repent and receive His forgiveness. Yet, after you have prayed with sincerity, if God does not reveal anything of this sort, and there doesn't seem to be any other reason for the difficulties you are having, you can suspect that Satan has constructed an obstacle in your life to contain the advancement of the kingdom that you are making or are about to make. You need a spiritual breakthrough. Follow the steps to receiving a spiritual breakthrough outlined in study 12. Wherever you are, the breakthrough is on its way. It will lead you out of your spiritual, personal, vocational, or ministerial stagnancy so that you can bring down the enemy's walls of containment, destroy the works of the devil, and advance God's kingdom.

+ If we do not establish God's authority in our lives and submit to His superior rule, we have no legal right to exercise His power. When the enemy doesn't see God's government in us, he challenges our authority and refuses to leave. Perhaps you have granted Satan the legal right to remain in your situation because you have not been yielded to God and His delegated human authorities. If you have been resisting God and living in rebellion, then repent and submit to Him and the people whom He has placed in authority over you. Receive God's forgiveness, and then move forward to advance His kingdom with authority and force!

+ Each of us needs to seek God earnestly to discern our "territory" and fulfill our particular assignment from Him. Sometimes, our assignment will involve being in full-time ministry; however, God calls believers to many fields, such as law, government, education, the arts, science, and engineering. If your life is not bearing fruit for God, or if your ministry is ineffective, ask yourself questions such as these: "To what territory, or sphere of influence, have I been assigned by God?" "Why am I in my present territory? Did I let circumstances lead me here? Did I come by my own choice? Or did God plant me here?" "Is my purpose connected to this territory?" "Who is my delegated authority—for example, my pastor or apostle? Am I allowing him to train, disciple, and guide me according to God's Word?" "Am I bearing the kind of fruit that lasts?" Pray about these questions, respond to what God tells you, and ask Him to confirm the territory and assignment He has given you. Once they are confirmed, ask God to fill you with His passion for kingdom expansion. Then, step out in faith to extend the kingdom in your territory.

ENCOUNTERS WITH GOD'S KINGDOM

Church Multiplies Members and Ministry After Spiritual Breakthroughs

Henry and Claudia González are pastors of a church in Colombia. At one time, their leadership was passive, and they felt spiritually weak. People seemed to leave their church as fast as they came. They also had been unable to break through in the area of miracles. Then they attended the Supernatural Fivefold Ministry School at King Jesus Ministry, and they received spiritual fatherhood and covering for their church. This resulted in a radical transformation in their ministry. They started with 600 people, and 120 of them left the church. However, after that, the congregation grew to more than 1,000 members with the addition of new believers. The church continues to grow, and the congregation's spiritual gifts have been activated. Furthermore, the church was able to pay off its mortgage in only six months!

During their regular services, God heals people who are suffering from cancer, leukemia, pulmonary disease, and many other sicknesses. One of the miracles that had the greatest impact was the resurrection of an eight-year-old named Denis hours after he was declared dead. His father had taken him to the doctor because he was complaining of leg pain. He was diagnosed with a malignant tumor on his femur. After further testing, the medical personnel discovered that his lungs had also been affected. The hospital called for a medical consultation, and they decided the femur had to be replaced. During the surgery, a complication arose, causing significant blood loss. The boy went into shock and died in the operating room. Two hours after all of Denis's vital signs had disappeared, the orthopedic surgeon, who was a Christian, prayed for him and rebuked the spirit of death. To the glory of God, he came back to life! Denis testified that while he was dead, he could see himself floating through the clouds with God the Father. New tests revealed that the metastasis in his lungs had reversed. God had not only breathed life back into Denis but also healed him of cancer.

As part of their church's multiplication, Henry and Claudia González have planted seven churches on donated land. At one of those locations, they had a warlock for a neighbor. The pastors decreed that the warlock would leave in one month. After a month, the wife and son of the warlock came to Christ, and, a month later, the warlock was also saved. Today, he is a transformed man, free of witchcraft.

These pastors testify, "Spiritual fatherhood released the inheritance of the supernatural and gave us security in God's purpose for our lives. It uprooted from us and from the church the passivity, the discouragement, and everything else that was holding us back, and it established His kingdom in our territory."

ANSWER KEY

Study 1: The Kingdom of God Is Within You

Part I: A Kingdom Bestowed from Heaven

1. *"Repent, for the kingdom of heaven is at hand."*

2. (a) not of this world; (b) not from here

3. the kingdom

4. *"…the kingdom of God is within you."*

5. They both sold all that they had in order to obtain it.

Part II: Qualities and Character of the Kingdom of God

6. in power, in the Holy Spirit, and with deep conviction

7. (a) by healing all kinds of sickness and all kinds of disease among the people; (b) by miracles, wonders, and signs, which God did through Him

8. righteousness; peace; joy

Part III: How to Enter the Kingdom of God

9. (a) He must be born of water and the Spirit. (b) We must confess with our mouth the Lord Jesus and believe in our heart that God raised Him from the dead. (c) received Him; believe in His name

10. Repent; Repent

11. to be converted and become as little children; (b) humility

Part IV: The Priority of the Kingdom

12. (a) *"Your kingdom come. Your will be done on earth as it is in heaven."* (b) on earth

13. (a) the kingdom of God and His righteousness; (b) *"All these things"* will be added to us. (c) food, drink, and clothing

14. a kingdom which cannot be shaken

15. (a) a wise man who built his house on the rock; (b) The house built on the rock did not fall. The house built on the sand fell.

Study 2: The Original Mandate of Dominion

Part I: Created to Have Dominion

1. in His own image and likeness

2. (a) Spirit; (b) the spirit

3. Be fruitful; multiply; fill the earth

4 good works

5. subdue it; have dominion over

6. the garden of Eden

Part II: Understanding Dominion

7. (a) wash one another's feet; (b) They lorded it over them and exercised authority over them. (c) *"Whoever desires to become great among you, let him be your servant. And whoever desires to be first among you, let him be your slave."*

8. (a) Resist the devil; (b) He will flee from us.

9. (a) He drove out of the temple those who bought and sold, and He overturned the tables of the money changers and the seats of those who sold doves. He would not allow anyone to carry wares through the temple. (b) *"Is it not written, 'My house shall be called a house of prayer for all nations'? But you have made it a 'den of thieves.'"*

10. forgive and comfort the man, lest he be swallowed up by too much sorrow, and reaffirm their love to him

11. so that they may be sound in the faith

12. for our profit, that we may be partakers of His holiness

Study 3: Dominion Relinquished and Regained

Part I: How Mankind Fell from Dominion

1. (a) the tree of life and the tree of the knowledge of good and evil; (b) *"Of every tree of the garden you may freely eat; but of the tree of the knowledge of good and evil you shall not eat, for in the day that you eat of it you shall surely die."*

2. "You must not eat from any tree in the garden."

3. (a) *"You will not surely die."* (b) Her eyes would be opened, and she would be like God, knowing good and evil.

4. (a) They ate the fruit. (b) not deceived; being deceived

5. (a) The ground was cursed, and Adam would toil to eat of it all the days of his life. The ground would bring forth thorns and thistles for him, and he would eat the herb of the field. He would eat bread by the sweat of his face, and when he died, his body would return to the ground from which it had been taken—he would return to dust. (b) death

6. *"Get behind Me, Satan! You are an offense to Me, for you are not mindful of the things of God, but the things of men."*

Part II: The Four Stages of Adam's Fall

7. the tree of the knowledge of good and evil

8. (a) in the image and likeness of God; (b) the idea that if they ate the fruit, their eyes would be opened, and they would be like God, knowing good and evil

9. The church tolerated a woman named Jezebel who called herself a prophetess. Her teaching was misleading people into sexual immortality and eating food sacrificed to idols.

10. (a) evil; (b) pride, arrogance, the *"evil way,"* and the perverse mouth

11. (a) being drawn away by our own desires and enticed; (b) sin; (c) death

Part III: The Catastrophic Result of Adam's Sin

12. (a) *"the ruler of this world"*; *"the god of this world"*; (b) Satan is a murderer and a liar. There is no truth in him. He is a deceiver. He comes to steal, kill, and destroy.

13. (a) as *"enmity against God"*; (b) the law of God; (c) *"For all have sinned and fall short of the glory of God."* (d) adultery, fornication, uncleanness, lewdness, idolatry, sorcery, hatred, contentions, jealousies, outbursts of wrath, selfish ambitions, dissensions, heresies, envy, murders, drunkenness, and revelries; (e) the kingdom of God

Part IV: Jesus Restored Humanity to Dominion

14. to destroy the works of the devil

15. (a) He quoted what is written in God's Word. (b) He left Jesus until an opportune time. (c) in the power of the Spirit

16. *"All authority has been given to Me in heaven and on earth."* (b) *"And I will give you the keys of the kingdom of heaven, and whatever you bind on earth will be bound in heaven, and whatever you loose on earth will be loosed in heaven."* (c) abundant life

Study 4: Jesus' Resurrection Established His Kingdom and Dominion Over the Kingdom of Darkness

Part I: Jesus Experienced Three Kinds of Death on Our Behalf

1. death

2. (a) crucifixion/He was crucified. (b) *"Father, into Your hands I commit My spirit."*

3. the iniquity of us all

4. Their iniquities had separated them from Him, and their sins had hidden His face from them, so that He would not hear.

5. *"My God, My God, why have You forsaken Me?"*

6. so that we might become the righteousness of God in Him

7. (a) "*...so will the Son of Man be three days and three nights in the heart of the earth.*" (b) "*You have laid me in the lowest pit, in darkness, in the depths. Your wrath lies heavy upon me, and You have afflicted me with all Your waves. You have put away my acquaintances far from me; You have made me an abomination to them; I am shut up, and I cannot get out.*"

8. "*For You will not leave my soul in Sheol, nor will You allow Your Holy One to see corruption.*"

Part II: Jesus Experienced Two Resurrections on Our Behalf

9. (a) by the Spirit; (b) by the glory of the Father

10. the spirits in prison

11. (a) those who are dead; (b) that they might be judged according to men in the flesh, but live according to God in the spirit

12. (a) the firstfruits of those who have fallen asleep; (b) the faithful witness, the firstborn from the dead, and the ruler over the kings of the earth

13. (a) into heaven; to the right hand of God; (b) the name that is above every name

14. (a) alive together with Christ; (b) We are raised up with Christ, and we sit together in the heavenly places in Him.

Study 5: A Revelation of the Resurrection for the Kingdom Here and Now

Part I: Ten Essential Revelations of the Resurrection

1. (a) The resurrected Jesus appeared and told Thomas to put his finger in the nailprints from His crucifixion, and his hand in the place where the soldier's spear had wounded His side. Then, He told Thomas not to be unbelieving but believing. Thomas responded, "*My Lord and my God!*" (b) "*Blessed are those who have not seen and yet have believed.*" (c) Peter told the lame man to rise up and walk in the name of Jesus, and he took him by the right hand and lifted him up. (d) His feet and ankle bones immediately received strength, and he was able to walk and leap as he praised God.

2. children of God

3. newness of life

4. Our faith would be empty; we would be found false witnesses of God; our faith would be futile; we would still be in our sins; those who had fallen asleep in Christ would have perished; our hope in Christ would be for this life alone, and we would be pitiable.

5. the Son of God with power; by the resurrection from the dead

6. (a) "*I am He who lives, and was dead, and behold, I am alive forevermore.*" (b) became a living being; became a life-giving spirit

7. (a) King of Kings and Lord of Lords; (b) He disarmed them, and He made a public spectacle of them, triumphing over them.

8. (a) we have redemption through His blood; the forgiveness of sins; (b) He will raise us up (with Jesus). (c) He will transform our lowly bodies so that they may be conformed to His glorious body.

9. (a) They will reign in life through Jesus Christ. (b) cast out demons; lay hands on the sick; and they will recover

10. (a) great power; (b) The Lord worked with them and confirmed the word through the accompanying signs.

Part II: How to Walk in the Power of the Resurrection

11. (a) *"If anyone desires to come after Me, let him deny himself, and take up his cross daily, and follow Me."* (b) not as I will; but as You will; (c) by walking in the Spirit

12. (a) Christ; (b) by faith in the Son of God, who loved us and gave Himself for us; (c) the things that are above, where Christ is, sitting at the right hand of God; (d) We are to set our minds on things above; we are not to set our minds on things on the earth.

13. the hope of God's calling and the riches of the glory of His inheritance in the saints

14. (a) the exceeding greatness of God's power toward us who believe; (b) *"I am the resurrection and the life."* (c) raise the dead

15. the life of every living thing and the breath of all mankind

16. (a) *"Do not weep; she is not dead, but sleeping."* (b) After making the mourners leave the room, Jesus took the girl by the hand and said, *"Little girl, arise."* Her spirit returned to her, and she immediately got up. (c) Lazarus's sickness was not unto death. It was for the glory of God, so that the Son of God might be glorified through it.

Study 6: The Spiritual Conflict Between Two Kingdoms

Part I: How the Kingdom of God Rules

1. the Father

2. (a) heirs; heirs of God; joint heirs with Christ; (b) we shall be like Him

3. the Helper, the Holy Spirit

4. (a) *"Now separate to Me Barnabas and Saul for the work to which I have called them."* (b) After fasting and prayer, they laid hands on Barnabas and Saul (Paul) and sent them away. (c) There was going to be a great famine throughout all the world. (d) They determined to send relief to the believers in Judea. (e) that the man had faith to be healed; (f) Paul told him in a loud voice, *"Stand up straight on your feet!"* The man leaped and walked.

5. (a) Matthew 16:24: *"If anyone desires to come after Me, let him deny himself, and take up his cross, and follow Me."* Matthew 11:28: *"Come to Me, all you who labor and are heavy laden, and I will give you rest."* John 7:37b: *"If anyone thirsts, let him come to Me and drink."* (b) be willing and obedient

Part II: How the Kingdom of Darkness Rules

6. (a) He blinds their minds. (b) He snatches away what was sown in their hearts.

7. *"sons of disobedience"*

8. sexual immorality, impurity, lust, evil desires and greed, which is idolatry

9. (a) a spirit of divination; (b) Paul said to the spirit, *"I command you in the name of Jesus to come out of her."*

10. trying to attain your goal by human effort

11. principalities, powers, rulers of the darkness of this age, and spiritual hosts of wickedness in the heavenly places

Part III: Four Results of Jesus' Victory Over Satan at the Cross

12. more than conquerors

13. He took from him all his armor in which he trusted, and He divided his spoils.

14. the belt of truth, the breastplate of righteousness, having our feet fitted with the readiness that comes from the gospel of peace, the shield of faith, the helmet of salvation, and the sword of the Spirit, which is the word of God

15. (a) the power of death; (b) He released us.

16. casting out demons by the Spirit of God

Study 7: The Gospel of the Kingdom Proclaimed in the Now

Part I: The True Gospel of the Kingdom Is One of Power and Revelation

1. the power of God to salvation for everyone who believes

2. (a) that you are turning away so soon; to a different gospel; (b) faith in Jesus Christ

3. (a) The word of the Lord was rare; there was no widespread revelation. (b) People cast off restraint.

4. apostles; prophets

Part II: Revelation Must Be Acted Upon

5. (a) *"If only I may touch His clothes, I shall be made well."* (b) She went behind Jesus in the crowd and touched His garment. (c) The flow, or *"fountain,"* of her blood dried up, and she felt in her body that she was healed. Jesus told her, *"Daughter, your faith has made you well. Go in peace, and be healed of your affliction."*

6. *"But only speak a word, and my servant will be healed. For I also am a man under authority, having soldiers under me. And I say to this one, 'Go,' and he goes; and to another, 'Come,' and he comes; and to my servant, 'Do this,' and he does it."* (b) *"Assuredly, I say to you, I have not found such great faith, not even in Israel!"* (c) He was healed that same hour.

Part III: Stewards of God's Revelation

7. (a) through the revelation of Jesus Christ; (b) now has been made manifest; (c) my gospel; (d) the prophetic Scriptures

8. that he be found faithful

Part IV: Preaching the Gospel with Supernatural Evidence in the Now

9. (a) The gospel of the kingdom would be preached in all the world. (b) as a witness to all the nations

10. *"The blind see and the lame walk; the lepers are cleansed and the deaf hear; the dead are raised up and the poor have the gospel preached to them."*

11. signs and wonders, various miracles, and gifts of the Holy Spirit

12. (a) by what he had said and done; (b) signs and wonders, through the power of the Spirit of God; (c) fully proclaimed the gospel of Christ

Part V: Principles of Our Kingdom Commission

13. (a) *"Go therefore and make disciples of all the nations, baptizing them in the name of the Father and of the Son and of the Holy Spirit, teaching them to observe all things that I have commanded you."* (b) Go. (c) The Lord worked with them and confirmed the word through the accompanying signs.

14. (a) *"The harvest is plentiful, but the workers are few."* (b) for the Lord of the harvest to send out workers into His harvest field; (c) that no one should perish, but that all should come to repentance

15. (a) his brother Simon; (b) He brought Simon to Jesus.

16. (a) the synagogues; (b) Gentiles, kings, and the children of Israel; (c) Crispus, who was the ruler of the synagogue, and all his household; many of the Corinthians

Study 8: The Restoration of the Supernatural in the Church

Part I: Principles of the Supernatural

1. (a) Spirit; (b) *"I AM WHO I AM."* (c) the Beginning and the End; the Almighty; (d) *"God is not a man, that He should lie, nor a son of man, that He should repent. Has He said, and will He not do? Or has He spoken, and will He not make it good?"*

2. (a) *"He is before all things, and in him all things hold together."* (b) the word of His power

3. (a) He changes the times and the seasons; He removes kings and raises up kings; He gives wisdom to the wise and knowledge to those who have understanding; He reveals deep and secret things. (b) life, breath, and all things; (c) their preappointed times and the boundaries of their dwellings; (d) that they might seek Him and perhaps reach out for Him and find Him

4. *"gold or silver or stone, something shaped by art and man's devising"*

5. (a) the miracles and signs that Philip did; (b) He offered the apostles money and said, *"Give me this power also, that anyone on whom I lay hands may receive the Holy Spirit."* (c) because Simon thought the gift of God could be purchased with money; (d) Simon was poisoned by bitterness and bound by iniquity.

6. without limit

7. forever and ever

8. (a) love him; manifest Myself to him; (b) the works that He had been doing, and even greater works

9. (a) *"And on My menservants and on My maidservants I will pour out My Spirit in those days; and they shall prophesy. I will show wonders in heaven above and signs in the earth beneath: blood and fire and vapor of smoke. The sun shall be turned into darkness, and the moon into blood."* (b) We are not to be troubled. (c) peace

Part II: Opposition to the Supernatural

10. (a) that Jesus is the Christ; that Jesus Christ has come in the flesh; (b) our anointing from the Holy One; (c) *"having a form of godliness but denying its power"*

11. (a) *"Beware lest anyone cheat you through philosophy and empty deceit, according to the tradition of men, according to the basic principles of the world, and not according to Christ."* (b) foolish; (c) the power of God and the wisdom of God; (d) by casting down arguments and every high thing that exalts itself against the knowledge of God, and by bringing every thought into captivity to the obedience of Christ

Part III: Why We Need the Supernatural

12. (a) power and authority over all demons and diseases; (b) They departed and went through various towns, preaching the gospel and healing everywhere. (c) Many of them believed in the Lord.

13. (a) by abiding in Him; (b) that they would prosper in all things and be in health, just as their souls prospered

14. (a) a plowman overtaking a reaper, and a treader of grapes overtaking him who sows seed; (b) three thousand; (c) five thousand; (d) multitudes

15. (a) all things are possible; (b) *"Did I not say to you that if you would believe you would see the glory of God?"*

16. (a) whoever is born of God; whoever believes that Jesus is the Son of God; (b) our faith; (c) *"I can do all things through Christ who strengthens me."*

Study 9: A Dominion of Kings and Priests

Part I: The Covenant-Kingdom Connection

1. (a) a special treasure to Him above all people; a kingdom of priests and a holy nation; (b) has made us kings and priests to His God and Father

2. the head and not the tail; above only, and not beneath

Part II: The Priestly Ministry of Christ

3. Apostle; High Priest

4. the order of Melchizedek

Part III: The Role of Priest in God's Kingdom in the Now

5. (a) holy; acceptable to God; (b) Jesus Christ; (c) resist conforming to this world and be transformed by the renewing of our minds; (d) the good and acceptable and perfect will of God

6. (a) because He is great and most worthy of praise; (b) continually

7. (a) *"Love your enemies, do good, and lend, hoping for nothing in return."* (b) A good measure, pressed down, shaken together, and running over, will be given back to us. (c) The generous person will prosper; the person who refreshes others will be refreshed.

8. (a) tithes and offerings; (b) *"Truly I say to you that this poor widow has put in more than all; for all these out of their abundance have put in offerings for God, but she out of her poverty put in all the livelihood that she had."* (c) Each one should give as he purposes in his heart, not grudgingly or out of necessity. (d) a cheerful one

9. (a) supplications, prayers, intercessions, and giving of thanks; (b) Verse 10: that God's kingdom would come and His will would be done earth as it is in heaven; verse 11: that God would give us our daily bread; verse 12: that God would forgive us our debts, as we forgive our debtors; verse 13a: that God would not lead us into temptation but deliver us from the evil one

10. a chosen generation; a royal priesthood; a holy nation; His own special people

Part IV: The Role of King in God's Kingdom in the Now

11. (a) *"The Lord shall send the rod of Your strength out of Zion."* (b) *"Rule in the midst of Your enemies!"* (c) In My name; (d) faith in Jesus' name

12. (a) They constantly offered prayer to God for him. (b) an angel of the Lord; (c) They were astonished. (d) An angel of the Lord immediately struck him down, because he did not give glory to God. He was eaten by worms and died. (e) It grew and multiplied.

13. (a) that if we ask anything according to His will, He hears us; (b) the petitions that we have asked of Him

14. (a) *"There shall not be dew nor rain these years, except at my word."* (b) shut up the heavens so that there be no rain; (c) *"Go, present yourself to Ahab, and I will send rain on the earth."* (d) *"Go up, eat and drink; for there is the sound of abundance of rain."* (e) The sky became black with clouds and wind, and there was a heavy rain. (f) with a nature like ours; (g) the effective, fervent prayer of a righteous man

15. (a) The place where they were assembled together was shaken, they were all filled with the Holy Spirit, and they spoke the word of God with boldness. (b) Through the hands of the apostles many signs and wonders were done among the people. Multitudes of both men and women were increasingly added to the Lord. People who were sick or tormented by unclean spirits were all healed.

16. We do not know what we should pray for, but the Spirit makes intercession for us with groanings which cannot be uttered; He makes intercession for us according to God's will.

Study 10: Faith: The Currency of the Kingdom

Part I: Where Faith Originates

1. *"the substance of things hoped for, the evidence of things not seen"*

2. by hearing, and hearing by the word of God

3. *"Man shall not live by bread alone, but by every word that proceeds from the mouth of God."*

4. a measure of faith

5. what He sees the Father do; the Son also does in like manner

6. (a) death and life; (b) what is good for necessary edification, that it may impart grace to the hearers; (c) psalms, teachings, tongues, revelations, and interpretations

7. *"With God nothing will be impossible."*

Part II: How to Live and Move in "Now" Faith

8. (a) the just; (b) from faith to faith

9. (a) the end from the beginning; from ancient times things that are not yet done; (b) through faith and patience

10. He will guide you into all truth; He will tell you things to come

11. (a) light; understanding to the simple; (b) teaching, rebuking, correcting, and training in righteousness

12. (a) pull down strongholds; (b) by casting down arguments and every high thing that exalts itself against the knowledge of God; by bringing every thought into captivity to the obedience of Christ

13. (a) meditate on God's precepts, contemplate His ways, delight himself in His statutes, and not forget His word; (b) *"Open my eyes, that I may see wondrous things from Your law."* (c) *"Teach me, O Lord, the way of Your statutes, and I shall keep it to the end. Give me understanding, and I shall keep Your law; indeed, I shall observe it with my whole heart."*

14. The truth will make us free.

15. (a) *"By His stripes we are healed."* (b) *"And my God shall supply all your need according to His riches in glory by Christ Jesus."* (c) *"To console those who mourn in Zion, to give them beauty for ashes, the oil of joy for mourning, the garment of praise for the spirit of heaviness."* (d) *"Therefore we do not lose heart. Even though our outward man is perishing, yet the inward man is being renewed day by day. For our light affliction, which is but for a moment, is working for us a far more exceeding and eternal weight of glory, while we do not look at the things which are seen, but at the things which are not seen."*

16. (a) faith, virtue, knowledge, self-control, perseverance, godliness, brotherly kindness, and love; (b) We will be neither barren nor unfruitful in the knowledge of our Lord Jesus Christ.

17. (a) faith working through love; (b) the love of God

Study 11: Demonstrations of Kingdom Power Here and Now

Part I: Knowledge Should Lead to Supernatural Experience

1. does not understand it

2. (a) the word planted in us; (b) someone who looks at his face in a mirror and then goes away and immediately forgets what he looks like

Part II: The Balance Between the Spirit and the Word

3. (a) The Spirit of God hovered over the face of the waters. (b) He said, *"Let there be light,"* and there was light.

4. the Scriptures and the power of God

5. with a sound from heaven like a rushing mighty wind; with divided tongues, as of fire, which sat upon each of them; with the sounds of other tongues

Part III: Purposes of Demonstrating God's Kingdom Here and Now

6. in demonstration of the Spirit and of power

7. (a) things pertaining to the kingdom of God; (b) power from on high; (c) Those who received the word were baptized, and about three thousand souls were added to the number of Jesus' followers. (d) the healing of a man who had been lame from birth

8. (a) She had a spirit of infirmity, which caused her to be bent over and unable to raise herself up. (b) eighteen years; (c) Satan; (d) being a daughter of Abraham

9. (a) You; Father; are in Me; and I in You; (b) They would ask what they desired, and it would be done for them. (c) in them

10. (a) that they may be made perfect in one; that the world may know that You have sent Me; (b) *"For by one Spirit we were all baptized into one body; whether Jews or Greeks, whether slaves or free; and have all been made to drink into one Spirit."* (c) *"There are diversities of gifts, but the same Spirit. There are differences of ministries, but the same Lord."* (d) They should be reverent in their behavior, not slanderers, not given to much wine; they should be teachers of good things; they should admonish the young women to love their husbands and children.

11. (a) over all the power of the enemy; (b) They shall not prevail against it.

12. (a) the aroma of death leading to death; (b) the aroma of life leading to life; (c) *"They are new every morning."*

13. *"He who believes in Me, the works that I do he will do also; and greater works than these he will do, because I go to My Father."*

14. *"The kingdom of heaven suffers violence, and the violent take it by force."*

Study 12: Kingdom Expansion by Spiritual Force

Part I: We Must Have a Revelation to Go into All the World

1. *"Go into all the world and preach the gospel to every creature."*

2. a great persecution; went everywhere preaching the word

3. (a) a man traveling to a far country, who called his servants and delivered his goods to them; (b) a certain number of "talents," according to their ability; (c) He went on a journey. (d) *"Well done, good and faithful servant; you were faithful over a few things, I will make you ruler over many things. Enter into*

the joy of your lord." (e) "Take the talent from him, and give it to him who has ten talents." (f) more will be given; he will have abundance; even what he has will be taken away

Part II: The Enemy's Plan to Contain the Kingdom

4. (a) "Far be it from You, Lord; this shall not happen to You!" (b) "Get behind Me, Satan! You are an offense to Me, for you are not mindful of the things of God, but the things of men."

5. (a) He had prayed for Peter, so that his faith would not fail. (b) strengthen his brethren

Part III: Steps to Receiving a Spiritual Breakthrough

6. strong in the Lord and in the power of His might

7. (a) be sober and vigilant; (b) resist him, remaining steadfast in the faith; (c) perfect; establish; strengthen; and settle you

8. "In your anger, do not sin."

9. "For who is this uncircumcised Philistine, that he should defy the armies of the living God?"

10. (a) But Paul; greatly annoyed; (b) He commanded the evil spirit to come out of the girl in the name of Jesus.

11. (a) "The kingdom of heaven suffers violence, and the violent take it by force." (b) bind him

12. (a) a new song, a hymn of praise to God; (b) Many people would fear the Lord and put their trust in Him. (c) the good news of God's salvation; His glory among the nations; His wonders among all peoples; (d) "For He has done marvelous things; His right hand and His holy arm have gained Him the victory." (e) psalms, hymns, and spiritual songs; (f) sing and make melody to the Lord

Part IV: Demonstrate the Kingdom of Power Here and Now

13. (a) to bear fruit that remains; (b) He will give us whatever we ask Him in Jesus' name.

14. "But you shall receive power when the Holy Spirit has come upon you; and you shall be witnesses to Me in Jerusalem, and in all Judea and Samaria, and to the end of the earth."

15. "Enlarge the place of your tent, and let them stretch out the curtains of your dwellings; do not spare; lengthen your cords, and strengthen your stakes. For you shall expand to the right and to the left, and your descendants will inherit the nations, and make the desolate cities inhabited."

16. (a) "Of the increase of His government and peace there will be no end." (b) with judgment and justice

17. (a) "The kingdom of heaven is at hand." (b) healing the sick, cleansing the lepers, raising the dead, and casting out demons

ABOUT THE AUTHOR

Apostle Guillermo Maldonado is a man called to bring God's supernatural power to this generation at the local and international levels. Active in ministry for over twenty years, he is the founder and pastor of Ministerio Internacional El Rey Jesús [King Jesus International Ministry]—one of the fastest-growing multicultural churches in the United States—which has been recognized for its development of kingdom leaders and for visible manifestations of God's supernatural power.

Having earned a master's degree in practical theology from Oral Roberts University and a doctorate in divinity from Vision International University, Apostle Maldonado stands firm and focused on the vision God has given him to evangelize, affirm, disciple, and send. His mission is to teach, train, equip, and send leaders and believers to bring the supernatural power of God to their communities, in order to leave a legacy of blessings for future generations. This mission is worldwide. Apostle Maldonado is a spiritual father to more than 100 pastors and apostles of local and international churches as part of a growing association, the New Wine Apostolic Network, which he founded.

He has authored many books and manuals, a number of which have been translated into several languages. His previous books with Whitaker House include *How to Walk in the Supernatural Power of God* (*Cómo Caminar en el Poder Sobrenatural de Dios*), *The Glory of God* (*La Gloria de Dios*), and *The Kingdom of Power: How to Demonstrate It Here and Now* (*El Reino de Poder: Cómo Demostrarlo Aquí y Ahora*). In addition, he preaches the message of Jesus Christ and His redemptive power on his international television program, *Tiempo de Cambio* (*Time for Change*), which airs on several networks, thus reaching millions worldwide.

Apostle Maldonado resides in Miami, Florida, with his wife and partner in ministry, Ana, and their two sons, Bryan and Ronald.